Time as History

In *Time as History,* George Grant's 1969 Massey lectures, he reviews the thought of Friedrich Nietzsche and concludes that, since the modern age is preoccupied with the future and technical progress, people must turn back to the past in the hope of finding there what has been lost in the dynamic present. Grant was the first Canadian philosopher to pay serious attention to the thought of Nietzsche, and his analysis of the German philosopher forms the central focus of the lectures.

William Christian has restored material from the broadcast version of the lectures. His introduction places Grant's interest in Nietzsche in the perspective of the former's developing analysis of technology and draws extensively on Grant's unpublished notebooks and lectures.

WILLIAM CHRISTIAN is the author of *George Grant: A Biography,* and a professor in the Department of Political Studies, University of Guelph.

GEORGE GRANT

Time
as
History

Edited with an Introduction
by William Christian

UNIVERSITY OF TORONTO PRESS
Toronto Buffalo London

© University of Toronto Press 1995
Toronto Buffalo London
Printed in the U.S.A.

Reprinted 2001, 2017

ISBN 0-8020-0640-X (cloth)
ISBN 0-8020-7593-2 (paper)

Printed on acid-free paper

Originally published by the CBC Learning Systems 1969

Canadian Cataloguing in Publication Data

Grant, George, 1918–1988
Time as History

Text includes the version published by the CBC Learning Systems
as the text of the 1969 CBC Massey lectures 'Time as History',
passages from the broadcast version and the 6th program,
a dialogue between George Grant and Charles Malik.
ISBN 0-8020-0640-X (bound) ISBN 0-8020-7593-2 (pbk.)

1. Time.   2. History – Philosophy.   3. Nietzsche, Friedrich,
Wilhelm, 1844–1900 – Contributions in philosophy of history.
I. Christian, William, 1945– .   II. Title.

D16.9.G73 1995   901   C95-930480-0

University of Toronto Press acknowledges the financial assistance to its
publishing program of the Canada Council and the Ontario Arts Council.

Contents

Editor's Introduction:
George Grant's Nietzsche

A few months before Grant's last illness, I sent him a copy of
a work by Jacques Derrida. He knew the influential French
deconstructionist by reputation, but had never read any of his
books. Derrida's extensive influence throughout Europe and
America was evidence of the spread of Nietzsche's influence
and that of his epigones. Indeed most of those who had lis-
tened to the original broadcasts of 'Time as History' and most
who read the lectures in their printed form, Grant believed,
were unconscious Nietzscheans, although they had probably
imbibed their Nietzsche through writers such as Derrida or
Freud or Max Weber, rather than directly. Nietzsche was in
the intellectual air we breathed, and his thought determined
ours all the more effectively because we had not thought
through, as Nietzsche had (with what Grant always called 'con-
summate clarity'), the implications of his novel vision of
human beings and human life. As moderns, especially as modern North Americans, we simply take for granted that time is
history and we live our lives beyond good and evil (that is,
oblivious of eternity), unaware of the moral abyss into which
we are falling.

A Family History of a Family of Historians

When George Grant died in Halifax in 1988 his obituarists remembered him as the celebrated author of *Lament for a Nation* (1965) and *Technology and Empire* (1969). He was, in their view, a Canadian nationalist, a fierce critic of modern technology and the country's most famous political philosopher. No one, it seems, remembered that Grant had started his intellectual life as an historian or that his transmutation into a philosopher took place slowly over several decades.

Yet he had come by his original interest in history quite naturally: it was one branch of the family business (education and politics were the others). His maternal grandfather, Sir George Parkin (1846–1922), was the author of a biography of Sir John A. Macdonald. George Monro Grant, his paternal grandfather and the celebrated principal of Queen's University, had published *Ocean to Ocean* (1873), the diary of the journey across Canada he made with Sir Sandford Fleming. Towards the end of his life G.M. Grant also published *French Canadian Life and Character, with historical and descriptive sketches of the scenery and life in Quebec* (1899).

William Grant, George Grant's father, was the most distinguished historian of the family. Trained in history at Queen's University, he went to Oxford to study Greats (classics). From 1906 until 1910 he lectured in colonial history at Oxford; then he returned to teach history at Queen's. Among his publications were a biography of his father (1905), a controversial history of Canada for use in Ontario high schools (1914) and *The Tribune of Nova Scotia: A Chronicle of Joseph Howe* (1915). William Grant also volunteered for active service in the Kaiser's war and saw action in France, where he was seriously injured. This experience profoundly affected his son: 'My father was a Nova Scotian, who had grown up in Kingston, Ontario, and was essentially a very gentle, strong scholar, who I think, above all, was ruined by the First World War. He was ruined physically; he was terribly wounded. For these people, who had grown up in the great era of progress, to meet the holocaust of the trenches was terrible.'[1]

The First World War, perhaps even more than the Second, was the great historical event that most influenced Grant, even though he was born on 13 November 1918, two days after the armistice. From his own experiences in France William Grant had become very bitter about the useless slaughter of the war, and his interest in the new League of Nations in the 1920s and 30s reflected his desire to prevent the recurrence of such a tragedy. His son's opinions on international affairs while a student at Upper Canada College, and later at Queen's University, closely reflected his father's views.

At Queen's, Grant also followed in his father's footsteps, and chose history as his major subject. However, even as an undergraduate, he was drawn to grand themes, rather than to the minutiae of historical research. As he complained to his mother: 'Professor Trotter has set us a colossal essay that does not have to be in till February although the bibliography has to be in next week. We each handed in three subjects and he chose which was best. My preference was "The Colonial Policy of the Protectorate." I am going to do that one. He says it is too extensive and I will have to narrow down the field to such a topic as "Cromwell's policy in the West Indies." That kind of detailed history gets me down.'[2]

After he completed his studies at Queen's (and won the history medal), he headed for Oxford on a Rhodes scholarship to study law. He found his new subject exciting for the intellectual discipline it imposed, but tiresome because of its attention to detail and its indifference to broader questions. 'Law is incredibly complicated and as yet my rather feeble mind cannot face it. In some ways it is disappointing because it is merely stating the law never asking what it is (as the basis) never asking why it is, as it is, never asking what it ought to be.'[3] The excitement he found in the grander themes of philosophical history are clear in his reaction to meeting the English historian Arnold Toynbee. 'Toynbee is the colossal kind of person who makes one feel that even if civilization goes down now – it is merely temporary as there is something essentially a part of God in man's make up.'[4]

After service as an Air Raid Precautions warden during the German bombing of London, Grant returned home in February 1942 suffering from a nervous breakdown and tuberculosis. He spent most of the next year recovering in bed. In 1943 he published a pamphlet, *Canada – An Introduction to a Nation.* In 1945 he addressed the same theme in *The Empire, Yes or No?* When he returned to Oxford after the war he decided to study theology, but he earned a little extra money by writing historical articles on Canada for *Chambers's Encyclopedia.* As he later explained to a student group: '... before I became a philosopher I studied history and still think very much as an historian.'[5]

The type of history to which he was increasingly drawn, however, reflected his early predispositions to the philosophy of history. This disposition was intensified by the study he made of philosophy after he was appointed to teach that subject in 1947 at Dalhousie University in Halifax, Nova Scotia. This concern is clear in his CBC radio address in praise of Charles Cochrane and his great work, *Christianity and Classical Culture.* 'Arnold Toynbee' he said, 'has just completed his mammoth *Study of History.* Rheinhold Niebuhr has written his *Nature and Destiny of Man.* But in Toynbee there is always a fuzziness about philosophic questions – a failure to analyse deeply. In Niebuhr there is a lack of subtlety – his answers are decisive but too easy. Beside either of them Cochrane is like a clear deep river, winding certainly to the sea. He goes right to the heart of the matter.'[6]

Grant himself tried to go right to the heart of the matter in his first major publication, *Philosophy in the Mass Age* (1959). In it he contrasted the Platonic view of time as the moving image of eternity with a rival understanding, which he called 'time as history': 'This view of time as history was brought out from the narrow confines of the Jewish people into the main stream of western civilization by Christianity. This is what the doctrine of the Trinity is: it incorporates into the timeless God of the Greeks, the God of project and of suffering; that is, the God of love. The sense of the unique importance of historical events was made absolute by the Incarnation. Our redemption has been achieved once and for all in His passion and death. This was not going to be repeated an infinite number of times. It was a unique and irreversible event.'[7]

Throughout the 1950s, Grant was deeply engaged with the thinker who had brought the concept of time as history into Western thought, G.W.F. Hegel.[8] He had hitherto accepted the general interpretation of Hegel advanced by his Dalhousie colleague and friend James Doull and by Oxford philosopher Michael Foster. However, Emil Fackenheim, a philosopher at the University of Toronto, had drawn his attention to the writings of Leo Strauss, and through Strauss, he encountered the great Hegelian interpretation of Alexandre Kojève,[9] in whose writings he discovered an explanation of the expansionary politics of global imperialism. During the 1960s Grant began with increasing urgency to consider the impact of this development, the spread of modern technological civilization throughout the world, most especially as it had taken shape in North America. *Lament for a Nation* (1965) was in part an attempt to show how the disappearance of Canadian sovereignty was the result of the movement in history towards what Grant, following Kojève, called 'the universal and homogeneous state.' He not only warned his fellow citizens of the destruction of their country's independence, but also attacked the spread of American civilization around the globe, most particularly in his opposition to the increasing American involvement in Vietnam.

The Vietnam War, he was slowly coming to understand, took on its terrifying dimension because it arose out of a new understanding of the nature of human existence. In *Philosophy in the Mass Age* Grant had come to see time as history as a direct development from the biblical account of time. He attributed his radical new insight in part to his friend the poet Dennis Lee, who, he wrote, 'understood that at the heart of our civilization lay an affirmation about "being" which was that civilization's necessity. The rampaging decadence of imperial war was not to be explained (within liberalism) as an aberration of our good system; it was not to be explained (within marxism) as something understood in terms of the dynamics of capitalism. In the very roots of Western civilization lay a particular apprehension of "being." '[10] Grant now knew that his task was to understand this particular vision of what it was to be human and how it had come to dominate in North America.

Friedrich Nietzsche

When the CBC invited Grant to deliver a series of radio lectures in 1969 (named the Massey lectures in honour of Grant's uncle, former Governor-General Vincent Massey),[11] he decided to focus on the thought of the nineteenth-century German philosopher Friedrich Nietzsche. He had come to the conclusion that Nietzsche's philosophic insights, more than any other thinker's, illuminated the background against which modern events, such as the Vietnam War and the growing Americanization of the Canadian economy, were moving. His task was to develop his insights in a form that would make them accessible to a large radio audience.

It was his son William, as he put it in the dedication to *Time as History*, who taught him to read Nietzsche. The dedication may have been meant more affectionately than literally. William, like so many young men and women in the sixties, was spiritually troubled by the world in which he lived. One of the thinkers he happened upon, in his last year of high school, was Nietzsche, and he was immediately and intensely excited by the ideas he found there. So that he could discuss his son's new enthusiasm, Grant began to reread Nietzsche. To his surprise he discovered a thinker who threw a brilliant light on the character of the very technological modernity he himself had been trying to understand for the past two decades.

In a sense Nietzsche was an intellectual acquaintance of long standing. Shortly after Grant's twenty-first birthday, while he was still a student at Balliol College, Oxford, he read *Thus Spoke Zarathustra* and wrote to his mother that Nietzsche had been completely misunderstood by most people: 'To say that he was the forerunner to such bestiality & cruelty as the Nazis is absurd. "I love him whose soul is deep even for wounding & whom a slight matter may destroy." "Pity is the cross upon which he is nailed who loveth mankind." That kind of thing is not like what he is supposed to be. He uses the theory of the "blond animal" in utter derision; yet people say that that is the basis of Nazidom.'[12]

It was a decade before Grant referred to Nietzsche again, and only in passing in his doctoral thesis on the thought of the Scottish Presbyterian theologian John Oman. Although he described Nietzsche as an instance of 'pagan irrationalism,' he compared his thought favourably with 'the post-war daemonisms' of Céline or D.H. Lawrence.[13] However, he curtly dismissed Nietzsche's attack on Christian morality in the following words. 'It also hardly seems worth noting in 1950 that Oman in dealing with Jesus as our ethical Lord makes short shrift of ideas such as Lawrence's and Nietzsche's that poverty of spirit means the morality of the slave. Presumably such ideas were more current among European intellectuals in his day than this.'[14]

Nietzsche, Grant slowly came to understand throughout the 1950s, was not revered by North American thinkers, but those he had influenced were. Grant had turned his attention in the mid-1950s to the French writer and thinker Jean-Paul Sartre,[15] who had been influenced by Nietzsche's greatest twentieth-century student, the German philosopher Martin Heidegger. He had also begun to wrestle with the impact of Freud on modern psychology,[16] and that of Max Weber on modern sociology and the practice of social work.[17] By 1962, when he delivered a CBC radio lecture on the psychoanalyst C.G. Jung, he had begun to consider Nietzsche's influence more explicitly. 'It is surely no accident that Jung grew up in that Germanic generation which was so deeply shaped by Nietzsche. For Nietzsche's attack on Semitic religion went more to the heart than any other of the many attacks which have characterized the last centuries; and it was made exactly at this point – man should pass beyond good and evil.'[18] Thus when Grant's friend James Doull wrote to him in 1968 about 'Heidegger and Nietzsche, who have drawn your attention anew' as authors who need 'far better interpretation than they have had,'[19] even he did not know that Nietzsche's thought had been percolating in Grant's brain for almost thirty years.[20]

Grant's key insight between the time he wrote *Philosophy in the Mass Age* and *Time as History* was that our conception of history had decisively changed over the past hundred years. The Platonic idea of time as the moving image of eternity had been replaced, as he had argued in the earlier radio lectures, by the idea of history as a process within which events took place. Moreover, for the earlier historicists, such as Marx and Hegel, the process as a whole took its meaning from the end towards which it aimed, and thus gave individual events their meaning in terms of that end. However, Nietzsche was more radical; for him, events were merely episodic moments of pure becoming, and all meaning was subjective. As Grant explained in *Time as History*: 'History (call it, if you will, "process") is that to which all is subject, including our knowing, including God, if we still find reasons for using that word' (p 11).

George Grant was never a Nietzschean, although his praise for Nietzsche's brilliant analysis of the nature of modernity was at times so fulsome that some readers have been mislead; this was easily done because he had such an exceptional ability to articulate positions other than his own with ease and lucidity. Grant considered that Nietzsche's central thought (which is so familiar to us that it 'does not seem very new today') explained better than anything Grant had previously read why modern men and women seem unwilling to accept the old moral restraints of natural law. As he put it in the broadcast version of the fifth lecture: 'Nietzsche thinks what it is to be a modern man more comprehensively, more deeply, than any other thinker, including Marx, including Freud, including the existentialists, including the positivists.' Nietzsche excelled all these others because, in recognizing and preaching the historical sense, he had declared that all frameworks, all perspectives, were human creations. He called these 'horizons,' and announced that all they had ever done in the past was to express 'the values that our tortured instincts will to create' (p 40). The most important and enduring of all these horizons had been God, but Nietzsche had declared that the horizon known as God was dead to Western human beings; that is, the morality, religion, and law that historically had given meaning to human life no longer did so. But Nietzsche was not a simple atheist of the Enlightenment who believed that once the infamous thing had been erased all would be well; he accepted that the death of God, although it made possible the complete liberation of human beings, also posed enormous danger to the civilization that had discovered it.

North America, Grant now came to understand, was a progressive civilization, 'a dynamic civilization and that dynamism has been related to the fact that our apprehension of temporality was concentrated on the future' (p 20). As the purpose of existence became more opaque, human beings increasingly sought to control their existence through a science that mastered and controlled nature: 'Their concentration on mastery eliminated from their minds any partaking in time other than as future' (p 20). In North America the Puritan emphasis on willing, which it took from the biblical tradition, 'was experienced as a pure potentiality' (p 20). North America became the realm of resolute willing, a place where we were, above all, determined to impose our stamp on existence. 'The will to change the world was a will to change it through the expansion of knowledge' (p 25).

Those in power in North America, Grant generalized, did not believe that it was possible to discover transcendent truths about how human beings should live. In the absence of such knowledge, they adopted what they sincerely believed was the only option for humanity – a creative plan to master the planet. For these moderns, 'changing the world becomes ever more an end in itself' (p 27). The person who had 'thought the conception of time as history more comprehensively than any other modern thinker before or since' (p 32) was Nietzsche. And he had also understood better than anyone else 'the profundity of the crisis that such a recognition must mean' (p 32).

Previous thinkers such as Hegel and Marx had celebrated history, while also preserving a concept of human nature. Nietzsche, in Grant's view, exploded the inadequacy of their attempt. Grant quoted Nietzsche's aphorism from *Human, All Too Human*: 'Lack of historical sense is the inherited defect of all philosophers' (p 36). Charles Darwin had taught that species of animals are in continual change: they come into being and pass away. Nietzsche took the radical step of extending the idea of constant change to human beings. As Grant explained: 'What is fundamental about all human behaviour (including our understanding of it – itself a behaviour) is its historicity.' There was, therefore, nothing stable or enduring either in nature or in us. 'It is the apprehension that in the shortest moment we are never the same, nor are we ever in the presence of the same. Put negatively, in the historical sense we admit the absence of any permanency in terms of which change can be measured or limited or defined' (p 37).

In the fourth lecture of *Time as History* Grant turned to the works of Nietzsche's maturity – *Thus Spoke Zarathustra, Beyond Good and Evil,* and *The Genealogy of Morals* – to explore the implications of this discovery for North America, whose destiny it was, Grant continued to affirm, to experience modernity in its fullest development. The discovery that time was history and nothing more was a discovery of great danger because it completely hid the last residual traces of the old tradition. These had been found in modern movements of progress such as liberal democracy and social democracy, which were the secular inheritors of the belief that there was some fundamental way in which all human beings were equal. The Christian tradition had affirmed the equality of human beings, since each human being possessed a soul. The death of God makes the basis of equality problematic. Grant quotes the famous passage in *Thus Spoke Zarathustra* to make his point: 'The masses blink and say: "We are all equal. – Man is but man, before God – we are all equal." Before God! But now this God has died' (p 43).

Marx and Hegel had put a 'net of inevitable success' under the actors in their historical drama. For them, although the process of bringing history to fulfilment might involve pain and sacrifice, the actions of human beings are guaranteed from the ultimate anguish' (p 48). However, if we are the creators of history, there is no inevitable outcome. The last men, as Nietzsche called the banal pleasure seekers, or the nihilists who prefer to will destruction rather than not willing at all, may be in charge of the earth 'for centuries and centuries' (p 48).

It is our fate, then, to live in a civilization that conceives time as history. Yet this fate, Grant affirms, is not 'one in which I think life can be lived properly. It is not a conception we are fitted for' (p 58). Nietzsche thought that it was, if only we could learn to love our fate, to overcome revenge, and to make our willing take place out of a positive love of the earth. Grant finds Nietzsche's call to will out of love of the earth inadequate: 'I do not understand how anybody could love fate, unless within the details of our fates there could appear, however rarely, intimations that are illumined; intimations, that is, of perfection (call it if you will God) in which our desires for good find their rest and their fulfilment' (p 60).

In the phrase 'intimations of perfection,' Grant was alluding to St Anselm's celebrated ontological argument,[21] the argument for the existence of perfection. Grant, in fact, accepted St Anselm's argument as the only valid proof of God's existence; and it was of central importance because it led to the conclusion 'that human beings are not beyond good and evil and that the desire for good is a broken hope without perfection, because only the desire to become perfect does in fact make us less imperfect' (p 60). However, Grant also knew that his personal and philosophic beliefs were not widely shared by his contemporaries. Their belief that it was possible to live decent lives outside this knowledge meant, in Grant's words, that 'the present darkness is a real darkness' (p 68) because the 'enormous corpus of logistic and science of the last centuries' had separated us from 'those images of perfection that are given us in the Bible and in philosophy' (p 68).

Yet a sun hidden by the clouds is still in the sky. Although it is difficult to see it, we need some point, however obscured, by which to orient ourselves in the world because, as individuals, we are called upon to make moral choices, and those choices will be all the harder since we live in a world that has given itself to dynamic willing. For Grant the Vietnam War was both symbolic and symptomatic of the type of moral crisis to which we would increasingly find ourselves called upon to respond. 'This is the crucial question about citizenship in this era: What is it to be a citizen in this new society ruled by its technical apparatus?'[22] It was hard, he told the idealistic students at the 1965 teach-in at the University of Toronto, to fight such a vast, imperial power-structure. But it was as necessary as it was liable to fail. The following words were an

injunction to guide each individual who lived in modern technological civilization: 'I am not advocating inaction or cyni-
cism. Nothing I have said denies for one moment the nobility
of protest. Nothing I have said denies that justice is good and
that injustice is evil and that it is required of human beings to
know the difference between the two. To live with courage in
the world is always better than retreat or disillusion.'[23]
Grant's writings, *Time as History* among them, often strike
readers as bleak and austere. In frustration, they attack Grant
for offering no solution, no guide to action. Yet Grant con-
stantly affirmed that he was not a pessimist, that no one who
believed in God could possibly be a pessimist. In an aside in
Time as History he noted that 'the absence of all nets is a truth
that those of us who trust in God must affirm' (p 48). Even
faced with the abyss, it was always open to each of us at every
moment to think and love what is good. That possibility might
not seem like much, but fortunately, it was enough. God was
always there if we chose to turn to Him. 'It may be that at any
time or place, human beings can be opened to the whole in
their loving and thinking, even as its complete intelligibility
eludes them' (p 68).

New and Uncertain Thoughts:
Grant's Later Nietzsche Seminars

Publication of *Time as History* was delayed until 1971 because Grant was seriously injured in an automobile accident
while on vacation in Barbados in May 1970. As a consequence
of his stay in hospital and his long convalescence at home, the
text of the published lectures was substantially the same as the
broadcast version. However, Grant was not yet content that he
had come fully to terms with Nietzsche's enucleation of modernity.

Grant was very conscious that he taught in a religion rather
than a philosophy department, but, as he understood it, that

position made it even more appropriate that he address Nietzsche's thought. For Grant, modernity, with its drive to dominate human and non-human nature, was the new religion of
North America. The religion of progress, which originated as
an outgrowth of secularized Christianity, was the unquestioned faith that bound most North Americans together. It was
a new religion and it had definitively replaced Christianity as
the dominant faith.[24] It was therefore not just appropriate, but
necessary, to explore the thought of Nietzsche who, although
he too rejected the doctrine of progress in its Enlightenment
form, had thought through the implications of the new faith
most clearly.

Grant began his 1969–70 Nietzsche seminar by reading his
Massey lectures and making a typewritten version available to
his students. However, as always, he intended in his seminars
to explore matters with which he had not dealt in his published work. As he explained to his students: 'Let me say in
parenthesis that what I am certain about I generally write down
and do not repeat in this class. I do not repeat them [sic] in
class because I think it impertinent to you to repeat what you
can read of mine in print if you so desire. Professors who go
on repeating their books in a class are a bore; people who
need that should just read the books. It is one's new and therefore uncertain thoughts one should give in class.'[25]

The new theme Grant wanted to explore was Nietzsche's
fundamental criticism of the 'tradition of revelation (faith) and
metaphysics (reason) in the West.'[26] Grant accepted the dominant Western position that it was impossible to do theology
without metaphysics. However, the meaning of one of the
important terms in this equation had drastically changed: the
modern understanding of reason, originating with Descartes
and culminating in Nietzsche's 'supreme attack on theology'
had overwhelmed the ancient understanding of reason, which
had been brought to its highest and clearest point in Christianity, particularly by St Augustine. In contrast, the modern ac-

count of reason 'tells us we must be atheists.'[27] In Grant's view, most contemporary theologies, both Catholic and Protestant (including philosophers such as A.N. Whitehead) are necessarily incoherent 'because they do not come to terms with what Nietzsche says.'[28]

The classical account of reason, by itself, did not necessarily lead to theism: 'Obviously Aristotle was no theist.'[29] Reason had to be understood, Grant argued, in its Platonic version, and that was a long and difficult endeavour. It was equally a necessary one, especially for those in the English-speaking tradition, because the English-speaking peoples had evaded the question by falling back on their faith in liberalism, but that liberalism was now totally riddled with contradictions.[30]

The theoretical and practical inadequacy of modern liberalism was to take on increased urgency when his wife, Sheila, drew his attention to the landmark American Supreme Court decision delivered by Mr Justice Blackmun in *Roe v. Wade* (1973). Sheila Grant had been active in the right-to-life movement, and her concern about the implications of the American decision brought Grant into the controversy. He addressed the question directly in the Wood Lectures entitled 'English-Speaking Justice,' delivered at Mount Allison University in Sackville, New Brunswick, early in 1974.[31] That legal judgment, with its denial of rights to foetuses, was for him a symbol of the theoretical and practical confusion into which the English-speaking world had fallen as a consequence of its acceptance of the modern doctrine of rationality.[32]

When he addressed the problem of Nietzsche again in his 1974–5 graduate seminar, therefore, the matter was, for him, an increasingly urgent one, and he gave the course jointly with the department of political science, as he explained, because 'it seems to me unwise to divorce the question of what constitutes the good political order and what it is proper for human beings to reverence.'[33] Human beings, as beings open to the whole, unavoidably needed to face the question of what constitutes the good life, and this question faced modern men and women as beings who inhabited a 'world-wide society based on the pursuit of the conquest of human and non-human nature.'[34] The possibility of such a society was known to the ancients, particularly Plato, but he 'turned away from such a society as not conducive to human good.' The novelty lay not in the potentiality of such a society, but in its actuality. It was Nietzsche, Grant declared, even more than his great predecessors Kant and Hegel, or his only great epigone, Heidegger, who had 'thought what is being thought in that modernity more comprehensively and completely than any other thinker.'[35]

In the older tradition, a 'truth' was an affirmation about existence. In the modern tradition, truth was a value and value was something created by human beings. But human beings need horizons in order to live, and the truth taught by modern science was that there were no horizons, that there was no stable existence, no being – only becoming. Truth, thus conceived, was a devastating discovery for human beings; this kind of truth killed life, since in the flux of existence, there was no moral point by which human beings could orient themselves.

In Nietzsche's philosophy, Grant argued, the highest life was the life of freedom, but freedom requires that becoming somehow be stabilized. Such stability could be attained only by the imposition of will on nature. The positive consequence of this stabilizing of becoming was that it allowed human beings to establish the conditions that permitted human life. There was, however, a negative side. The exaltation of the value of truth in the Western tradition closed down the highest vision, the Dionysian vision, that is, life as tragedy. Unless truth as it was understood by modern science were overcome, the highest type of human being, the *Übermensch* (overman or superman) could not come to exist. Plato had taught that the height for human beings was philosophy; Nietzsche attacked philosophy in the name of tragedy and the possibility of the higher human being. To face the abyss of existence as tragedy is a tremendous and dangerous task 'because it might drive us mad – like it drove [Nietzsche] mad.'[36]

Although Grant had hitherto celebrated Nietzsche as the thinker who had most comprehensively thought about modern western civilization, he now no longer saw Nietzsche as the culmination of the Enlightenment. Nietzsche was not, in Grant's eyes, simply 'the thinker who catches the very swell of the ocean of modernity.' He was far more radical than that; he was someone who 'is not content to swim with that current – but [who wants to] find other currents than that.'[37] This rejection of progress put Nietzsche at odds with the great political movements of the nineteenth century, liberalism and marxism. Both these ideologies contributed to the popular atheism of the West in the name of liberating human beings from the dead hand of religious institutions; but Nietzsche saw that popular atheism was leading to the creation of a 'much lower type of man than was produced by the theism of the past. The death of God, according to Nietzsche, is opening up this great degradation of man – the last men who are lower than past men who lived under theism.'[38] Nietzsche's atheism, by pointing to the higher man, was thus fundamentally different from the atheisms that preceded it. His was a new, right-wing, atheism. Intellectually, it was more honest than the left-wing atheism it attacked; but left-wing atheism was 'morally preferable to the right-wing atheism, just because it is secular-ized Christianity and Judaism.'[39]

For Grant, following Leo Strauss's argument in his essay 'The Three Waves of Modernity,'[40] the critical development was the abandonment of the standard of nature as a transcendent source of the good for human beings. The first of Strauss's waves involved 'the rejection of the ancient account of nature conceived teleologically.'[41] Hobbes and Locke were the great thinkers in this development. For them, although they saw no ends or purposes given in nature, they still took nature as the standard from which we divine, albeit negatively, our knowledge of the just regime.'[42] The second wave of thinkers – Rousseau, and most of all, Kant, Hegel, and Marx – rejected nature as the standard 'in the name of the discovery of history as the standard.'[43] This development implied the understanding of human beings pre-eminently as 'free animals.'[44]

The third wave of modernity, which dominates contemporary thinking, rested on the assertion that 'history is not rational and cannot provide us with the standards from which we come to have knowledge of the just regime'[45] This last wave was inaugurated by Nietzsche, and led to the prevalence of a life-denying historicism in both scholarship and practical life. Hegel's thought (as well as Marx's and Mill's), whatever its high ideals, reinforced a dangerous momentum towards nihilism.

Nietzsche accepted the position that the truth about the highest matters is radically historical, and that there is therefore no truth that man can ever possess which will not prove to be in need of radical revision. However, in 'The Advantages and Disadvantages of History for Life,' he moved decisively beyond the Hegelian position when he recognized that the truth of historicism is deadly for human beings; in Grant's words, 'We cannot live on the basis of the purely personal and relative character of our principles.'[46]

The twentieth-century existentialists interpreted this aspect of Nietzsche's teaching in terms of the free project, of free creation. In this, Grant thought, they misunderstood Nietzsche who, in his 'great admiration for the Greeks' conceived of culture as idealized nature. The word 'nature' is, of course, notoriously ambiguous, and this ambiguity is also present in Nietzsche who uses the word in both its popular sense and also in a way uniquely his own. In his early work, Grant argued, Nietzsche accepted technology – the conquest of nature – and therefore espoused the modern position in his acceptance of the view that it was not possible to talk of the nature of human beings because human nature itself had been conquered. In

siding with the moderns in accepting that nature could not
impose limits on human action, Nietzsche decisively rejected
a view that lay at the core of ancient thought. In contrast with
modern egalitarianism, Plato and Aristotle saw the non-egali-
tarian society as natural, and in his later writings Nietzsche
sought to retain both views: he still wanted the modern conception of nature, but he wanted 'it in a way that will include
the order of rank against egalitarianism.'[47] This insistence on
order of rank created a central political difference between
Nietzsche and the exponents of both marxism and American
liberalism. But they all agreed on one important matter, namely
that the rule of human beings should replace the rule of chance.
The overcoming of chance in turn meant the technologized
society, 'the society dedicated to the conquest of human and
non-human nature.'

However important these political questions were, they
paled into insignificance compared to Nietzsche's great attack
on the division between thought and the saints, or 'if you prefer, between thought and charity.' Grant rejected the position
advanced by thinkers as diverse as Tertullian and Leo Strauss
that there was a great division between Athens (philosophy,
rationality) and Jerusalem (revealed religion, faith): 'I just
deny that division.'[48] Reason could always understand what
charity commanded. It was clear that Nietzsche rejected revelation, but how did he stand with regard to metaphysics? He
attacked 'what has been called in the tradition metaphysics,'
but his doctrine of the will to power seemed, and was so interpreted by Heidegger, as a metaphysical doctrine in its own
right.[49]

To understand Nietzsche's doctrine of the will to power, it
was necessary to resolve the question, Who is it that wills? This
brought Grant to consider the question of the self in Nietzsche's
thought, a topic 'deeper' than he normally raised in class.[50]

Nietzsche attacked not only the ancient, Platonic-Aristotelian,
doctrine of the soul, he also rejected the teaching of modern

philosophy from Descartes to Hegel, which spoke in terms of
ego and subject. The oldest tradition, which understood soul
as spiritual substance, stood in the way of modern science's
conquest of human and non-human nature, because its vision
entailed the unchangeability of this substance. Modern science
emerged when the soul was divided into two phenomena: (a)
the consciousness or ego, and (b) the body as matter or nature.
Animals were subject purely to mechanical processes. 'In the
case of some beings, perhaps only man, these mechanical processes are accompanied by consciousness.'[51] Nietzsche repudi-
ated this post-Cartesian view in a way that put him closer, in
some respects, to Plato than to Descartes or Kant. He did so in
the name of the subconscious, an aspect of human beings that
'can never be made conscious.'[52]

It was Sigmund Freud who popularized the concept of the
subconscious, but Freud's view departed from Nietzsche's.
Freud never said unequivocally that the subconscious could
never be made fully conscious. To the extent that Freud saw
psychoanalysis as a science, the movement of the subconscious
to consciousness was a process that, in principle, was capable
of infinite progress. Nietzsche's self was creative; indeed, it
usurped the role of the creator God. It was at heart something
mysterious: 'The self is the abyss of freedom in the soul.' By
the *Übermensch* or superman, Nietzsche meant nothing less than
'the mysterious self which has taken the place of the mysterious God.'[53]

As bodies, human beings are driven by their passions. This
was the teaching of a series of philosophers, of whom Grant
singled out Hobbes, Spinoza, Hume, and Montesquieu. The
key statement was Hume's affirmation that reason was, and
could only be, the slave of the passions, and by this he meant
that reason was a kind of calculation.

For Plato the conflict between the passions concerned a
contrariety towards the same object of desire, at its highest the
desire for the whole. The idea of the whole was accessible to

human beings, and the question facing us when we experienced contrariety of desires was, Which desire was rational? Happiness (in Greek, *eudaemonia*) was the soul at unity with itself 'because it partakes in that which is the source of all unity – the ἰδεα του ἀγαθου [the idea of the good].' Virtue was the state in which the passions find their proper and just order of 'subordination and superordination within the soul as a unity.'[54]

In the seventeenth and eighteenth centuries, modern philosophers rejected this concept of virtue in favour of the view that virtue was itself a passion, albeit a good passion. Thus altruism or compassion had to fight the bad passion of selfishness. Their conclusion was that history had shown that reason (understood in the Platonic way) in the hands of the philosophic few was simply not a secure and effective means to control the passions of the unphilosophic many. The triumph of virtue would occur only when human beings understood that virtue, too, was a passion. This led to the recommendation that the good passions must be emancipated so that they might prevail against the bad passions. For example, Hobbes argued that it was necessary to liberate the fear of violent death, because it was only on that basis that it was possible to build a fairly rational society. The good passions give reason the strength to triumph in society.

Nietzsche carried this argument further in a way that put him simultaneously closer to, and farther away from, Plato than his immediate predecessors. He was nearer to the extent that he thought that virtue, as sublimated passion, was the highest passion; it was something sublime. However, he was farther away from Plato because he thought that the virtues were something different in each human being. To Nietzsche their similarity was merely one of names and they had nothing to do with reason.

Both Nietzsche and his modern predecessors agreed that, to liberate the beneficial and virtuous passions, it was necessary to break with the very idea of tradition, a word Grant often used to mean religion ('tradition [call it if you will religion]').[55] Nietzsche not only started from the modern attack on religion, he understood the core of modernity better than its originators and, most important, he passed beyond them when he advanced his celebrated doctrine of the eternal recurrence of the identical.

The doctrine of eternal recurrence of the identical was Nietzsche's response to the modern attempt to overcome chance. As Grant had argued in *Philosophy in the Mass Age*, the redemption of the past, the overcoming of its suffering and follies, had, for Marx, depended on the fact that history was moving to a future in which exploitation and oppression would finally and forever be overcome. For Nietzsche, Marx's answer would not have sufficed, because it was still dependent on the spirit of revenge, revenge against the past. The will, however, is impotent against the past, because it cannot change it. 'The past is the very character of time itself – to pass away.'[56] What can the will do in order to counteract its defeat by time?

Now Nietzsche saw that the past fragmentedness of human beings could be overcome, not by the conquest of fragmentedness and chance but by redeeming them. This 'redemption consists in the willing of fragmentedness – the affirmation of chance.'[57] All previous thought, be it Plato's or be it Marx's, sought revenge on time. Plato, Nietzsche charged, had conjectured the eternal precisely in order to get his revenge on time. Platonism and Christianity had degraded nature by positing the supernatural out of a spirit of revenge against time. Even marxism and liberalism were tainted by revenge in all its corrosiveness; as 'progressive' theories, they looked to future progress to redeem the suffering and injustice of the past. Nietzsche soared above both marxism and liberalism because he was also 'aware that nothing that is not eternal can satisfy a thinking man.'[58]

To sum up. The superman becomes possible through deliver-
ance from the spirit of revenge, from every [need] for the eternal which is beyond the perishable. The flux is willed. Time
and the pasts are willed, and that means to will the return of the
past. Willing the eternal return is the peak of the will. Through
liberation from the spirit of revenge the will becomes properly
willed because it has freed itself from that which frustrates the
will.
    Now this does not mean that Nietzsche ceases to be a mod-
ern in that he abandons the will to the future. He wills the future
while willing the past – in one and the same act. But he passes
beyond the great progressives such as Marx because the willing the past means the return of the past. We will the future and
the past – but that is only possible if time is a circle, a recurrence of the past.[59]

Human beings have always resented the past conceived as
eternal becoming because such a concept entails their eventual
annihilation in death. Socrates had taught that philosophy was
the practice of dying. In Grant's words, 'philosophy is meditation upon the fact of our finitude – upon death.'[60] The Christian
tradition intensified this concern because at the centre of
Christianity was a death.[61] Spinoza, however, announced that
philosophy should not be a meditation on death, but upon life,
and in this he was followed by the great progressive thinkers
such as Marx.
    Nietzsche's doctrine of the eternal recurrence of the identi-
cal was his meditation on death, and it is precisely because he
brought 'meditation on death' back into philosophy that he
passed beyond modern thought. Surprisingly, Grant declared
that his sympathy lay somewhere between Nietzsche's teaching and the traditional understanding of the uniqueness of
Christ's crucifixion, which had been brought into Western
Christianity by St Augustine and spread throughout the world
by Calvinist Protestantism. He did not believe that the cruci-

fixion was a limited historical event; other revelations and re-demptions might be granted. For example, in India, Christ's name might be Krishna (or as Simone Weil says, 'Wherever there is affliction, there is the Cross').[62] Grant claimed that he always reminded himself of his disagreement with the doc-trine of the sacrifice, once offered,[63] when his Anglican vicar was reciting the prayer of consecration. 'Is Christianity funda-mentally committed to the unicity of the historical process? If so, one has to give up Platonism. I hope not, but I am not sure.'[64]

Grant found the doctrine of eternal recurrence of the identi-cal an attractive correction to the view of time as history: 'It is ... a doctrine of the trans-historical whole of nature.' However, it was not a fully satisfactory solution to the modern concep-tion of time because 'it is not in itself, nor is meant to be, a rational doctrine.' It is a strange mixture of the two – an enig-matic, that is allusive, vision. Above all, it is a teaching that concerns the universal, and it is precisely the lack of a vision of the eternal (Leo Strauss's oblivion of eternity) that stands at the centre of modernity. In the tradition, that is religiously, universality cannot be avoided because human beings are rational beings, 'and universality is *the* expression of our ration-ality.'[65] Nietzsche's doctrine of the eternal recurrence of the identical brought back a teaching concerning the trans-histori-cal whole of nature. But it did so at the level of nature, not at the level of reason.

At the level of reason, Nietzsche's perspectivism prevented an affirmation of transcendence. All knowledge serves histori-cally specific life and is, therefore, interpretation. Fundamen-tally, this teaching absolutely affirms the doctrine that all knowledge is creation. Modern social science, especially that deriving from Max Weber, has accepted this side of Nietz-sche's teaching, but in Grant's view, it has done so only par-tially. Nietzsche realized that it was impossible to claim his-torical relativism as an absolute truth. He also understood that historical relativism is a deadly truth. Most important, though, the objective truth of historicism 'call it if you will God is dead'⁶⁶ must itself be interpreted, and that interpretation can be either noble or base. The base interpretation is ordinary relativism; the noble one is creativity. Most social scientists think that the relativist interpretation is more scientific, but Nietzsche affirms that both the base and the noble interpretation are 'quite outside science.'⁶⁷ The noble interpretation of historicism is human creativity understood as the will to power, or one's own self-awareness of one's own creativity.

The heart of the noble teaching accepts that there is nothing eternal except individuals in their individuality, but it allows an infinite affirmation of life with all its sufferings and defects in a way that is not possible in the base interpretation. The superman makes the return to nature possible because he shares with the beasts something that distinguishes both from historical man – harmony and unity within the cycle of nature.

Nietzsche's thought is worthy of study because of the clarity with which he enucleated modernity. Yet Grant declared that he reacted to Nietzsche's philosophy with a 'limitless repugnance,' which he had never felt so strongly as during that year's course. 'Nothing could be more repugnant than the doctrine of human beings as creative – indeed of philosophy itself as creative'⁶⁸ Creativity, for Grant, always remained the unique prerogative of the Creator God.

The limitless repugnance

Nietzsche continued to occupy Grant's thoughts until his death in 1988, although he increasingly found Jean-Jacques Rousseau's writings, especially his *Discourse on the Origin of Inequality among Men*, more illuminating than Nietzsche as a source of the modern understanding of human beings as historical creatures. In 1981, he wrote to a friend: 'I am going to write a piece – a long one – called "History and Justice," which

is to go into a book called "Technology and Justice," which I
hope to publish next year. The piece on "history" will be about
Rousseau who I now see as as great a founder of modernity as
Nietzsche. I think I have at last seen with some clarity something I have never seen before as to what modern people mean
by "history."'[69]

However, he returned to Nietzsche when he began to study
Heidegger's four volumes of engaged commentary on Nietzsche's thought in an English translation.[70] As we have seen,
Grant kept his more uncertain thoughts to the privacy of his
classroom, only setting his ideas down for publication when
he was confident that he had thought through the matter with
sufficient clarity.

This was never a precipitous process and it took him almost
a decade to bring his thought about Nietzsche into its final
form in *Technology and Justice* (1986).[71] It had not even been
until 1979, four years after his Nietzsche seminar at McMaster
that he had brought himself to explain in public some of the
grounds for his repugnance for Nietzsche's doctrines in 'Nietzsche and the Ancients: Philosophy and Scholarship.'[72] The
first part of this article raised the question of historicism in the
context of Nietzsche's critique of Greek, especially Socratic,
rationalism. In the second part he explained why he found Nietzsche's writing unsatisfactory. Nietzsche, above all, provided
the 'root and branch' critique of the Platonic tradition. Grant,
in effect, proposed to return the favour. 'If I were not afraid of
being taken as an innocent dogmatist, I would have written
that one should teach Nietzsche within the understanding that
he is a teacher of evil.'[73]

Unlike those who reject Nietzsche because they find no
explicit teaching about justice in his writings, Grant affirmed
that such a teaching is 'at the very core of what he is saying.'[74]
And Grant found that teaching frightening. He quoted a frag-
ment from *The Will to Power* (1884) in which Nietzsche wrote:
'Justice as function of a power with all encircling vision, which

sees beyond the little perspectives of good and evil, and so has a wider advantage, having the aim of maintaining something which is more than this or that person.' What frightened Grant about this formulation was that it seemed to give an account of justice 'as the human creating of quality of life.'[75] However, such creativity amounts to abandoning the truth of the Platonic conception of justice as giving to others their due. It does so by suggesting that there are some human beings to whom nothing is due, other than perhaps extermination. More specifically, it affirms that there is nothing extrinsic that limits human creative potential, that puts any limit on what we may do in the pursuit of the great enterprise of creating a quality of life beyond the little perspectives of good and evil. 'Human beings are so unequal in quality that to some of them no due is owed.'[76] In the idea of the technological world, which is almost now fully incarnated, this stance is the full consequence of the oblivion of eternity which has taken hold of Western thought.

It was not until 1986 that Grant finally believed he had come to terms with Nietzsche's thought in such a fundamental way that he could reject its most fundamental conclusion: that the discoveries of modern science showed that God was dead, and that Christianity had produced its own gravediggers. This rejection took the form of 'Faith and the Multiversity,'[77] Grant's most profound critique of the modern project. Thinking the thought contained in Simone Weil's aphorism 'Faith is the experience that the intelligence is enlightened by love,'[78] Grant showed persuasively that the whole of modern science and the ethical relativism that gave it such power was fundamentally flawed by its failure to account for our undoubted experience that love exists in the world and that it enlightens us. 'Modern scientists, by placing before us their seamless web of necessity and chance, which excludes the lovable, may help to reteach us the truth about the distance which separates the orders of good and necessity.'[79]

Nietzsche had argued that the Christian doctrine of the importance of truth had created modern rationalism, and modern rationalism had made Christianity a doctrine that could no longer be true for modern human beings. Although Grant, as we have seen, accepted this account of modern philosophy and its impact on subsequent Western thought, he now concluded that Nietzsche was right only as an historian, not as a philosopher. Historically 'western Christianity simplified the divine love by identifying it too closely with immanent power in the world.'[80] Both the Protestant and Catholic streams of Christianity were now paying the price for that failure and, to that extent, Nietzsche was right. This was a conclusion to which Grant had come as early as 1969, when he told his class: 'It appears to me that it is just western Christianity, with its account of individuality, freedom and will, which leads straight to Nietzsche's formulation of the question ... Nietzsche does not seem to me anti-Christian, but his formulations seem to me to come out of western Christianity.'[81]

Nietzsche sought to redeem humanity by placing what, in the tradition, were called moral judgments beyond good and evil. Grant considered this an 'atrocious price' to pay. Fully aware of the implications of what he was doing, Nietzsche took the 'prodigious and, to some, unconscionable step of questioning western Christianity.'[82] However, for Grant it was only western Christianity, a particular, although dominant, version of the Christian faith that had been undermined. Ironically, Nietzsche had helped to make clear 'what western Christianity seemed to forget in its moment of pride: how powerful is the necessity which love must cross. Christianity did not produce its own gravediggers, but the means to its own purification.'[83]

Grant knew well from his own life how difficult it was to shake off the modern vision and to undertake the task of purification. He called the following statement, addressed to a class in 1969, 'the most intimate thing I have ever said in a class-room.' It was less a confession of failure than a statement, in response to Nietzsche, that he placed the life of charity, the life fully lived by a saint, above the life of reason or philosophy, his own life. Simone Weil, was in his view, a modern saint who had understood Christianity purely and had both expressed that understanding clearly in her philosophical writings and lived the life of renunciation to which her understanding of Christianity pointed. As Grant said then:

What is said in [Simone Weil's writings] seems to me the truth. That is, when the chips are down, this is what I think about what is, and no criticism of it has ever convinced me. Yet at the same time it is not something I am able to live by. That is, I obviously do not think it is true in the sense of truth in Plato, in which desire and reason must be one. That is, for ten years, I have been in the very horrible position of thinking this position to be true and yet turning away from it.

Why do I make this rather egocentric remark? Because the following is true: 'Human nature is so constituted that any desire of the soul in so far as it has not passed through the flesh by means of actions and attitudes which correspond to it, has no reality in the soul. It is only there as a phantom' [Simone Weil]. That is the supreme truth of Christianity – the Incarnation – everything divine has to come to us by passing though our flesh.

I think this doctrine to be true. I do not consent to it, because I do not consent to its passing through my flesh. Therefore, there is something very strange in my passing this doctrine on to you as true, when I do not consent to it in desire. Indeed, there is one saying in the Bible that is indubitable. 'It is a fearful thing to fall into the hands of the living God.'[84]

Nietzsche's writings, then, by no means fully represent a final truth. To understand what Grant thought to be the truth about the highest matters, one must turn to 'Faith and the Multiversity,' in *Technology and Justice* (1986), his attempt to show how he participated 'intellectually in the mystery of Christianity.'[85] Without an understanding of the role of Christianity in Grant's thought, all discussions of Nietzsche are not only partial but misleading.

William Christian
Guelph, Ontario
August 1994

NOTES

1 George Grant, interview with David Cayley, 1985
2 George Grant to Mother, 8 November [1937]
3 George Grant to Gerald Graham, 30 November [1939]
4 George Grant to Dear Mum [early 1940]
5 George Grant, 'Address to History Society, University of Toronto,' probably 1970
6 George Grant, 'Charles Cochrane,' *Anthology*. CBL, 26 October 1954
7 George Grant, *Philosophy in the Mass Age* (Toronto: Copp Clark 1959; rpt., with an introduction by William Christian, Toronto: University of Toronto Press 1995), ch 4
8 For a discussion of Grant's indebtedness to Hegel's thought and the importance of Grant's friend James Doull, see Christian, Introduction to *Philosophy in the Mass Age* (1995)
9 Alexandre Kojève, *Introduction à la lecture de Hegel* (Paris: Gallimard 1947)
10 George Grant, 'Dennis Lee – Poetry and Philosophy,' in Karen Mulhallen et al., eds., *Tasks of Passion: Dennis Lee at Mid-Career* (Toronto: Descant 1982), 230–1
11 His predecessors were all equally distinguished: Northrop Frye, Frank Underhill, C.B. Macpherson, John Kenneth Galbraith, Paul Goodman, Martin Luther King, Jr, and Dr Ronald Laing
12 George Grant to Maude Grant, 22 November 1939
13 George Grant, 'The Concept of Nature and Supernature in the Theology of John Oman,' (DPhil thesis, Oxford 1950), 26

14 Ibid., 170–1
15 George Grant, 'Jean-Paul Sartre,' *Architects of Modern Thought* (Toronto: Canadian Broadcasting Corporation, 1955), 65–74
16 George Grant, Conceptions of Health, in Helmut Schoek and James W. Wiggins, eds., *Psychiatry and Responsibility* (Princeton: D. Van Nostrand 1962), 117–34
17 George Grant, Value and Technology, *Conference Proceedings: 'Welfare Services in a Changing Technology'* (Ottawa: Canadian Conference on Social Welfare 1964), 21–9
18 George Grant 'Carl Gustav Jung,' in *Architects of Modern Thought*, nos. 5 & 6 (Toronto: Canadian Broadcasting Corporation 1962), 73–4
19 James Doull to George Grant, 11 October 1968
20 For Grant, such a period of contemplation was not unusual. He often thought about a writer for a decade or more before he was prepared to write down his thoughts on paper.
21 I think Grant would have been in substantial agreement with Iris Murdoch's argument in *Metaphysics as a Guide to Morals* (London: Allen Lane 1992), ch. 13, 'The Ontological Proof.'
22 George Grant, 'A Critique of the New Left,' in Dimitrios I. Roussopoulos, ed., *Canada and Radical Social Change* (Montreal: Black Rose Books 1973), 58
23 Ibid., 59
24 See 'Introduction' to 'Religion and the State,' in George Grant, *Technology and Empire: Perspectives on North America* (Toronto: House of Anansi 1969), 43–5. For Grant's account of how this new faith came to dominate in North America, see George Grant, *English-Speaking Justice* (Toronto: House of Anansi 1985), Part III.
25 George Grant, 'Notebook: Nietzsche starting with B[eyond] G[ood] and E[vil] Part 6.' The material in this notebook is fragmentary; that for 1974–5 is extensive. Grant's notebooks, which are written in McMaster University spiral-bound notepads, of the sort students use for taking lecture notes, contain both jottings and fully written-out lectures, which Grant would normally read at the beginning of a class. Because they are unpaginated and unpublished, I refer only to the notebook as the source. Peter Emberley and Arthur Davis plan to publish extensive selections from these notebooks in their edition of Grant's collected works.
26 Ibid.
27 Ibid.

28 Ibid.
29 Ibid.
30 Ibid.
31 Grant revised these lectures very thoroughly, and they were not published until January 1978, although they bear a 1974 publication date.
32 'The natural rights tradition derives from the natural law tradition, specifically the idea that humans receive or consent to order. Dynamic willing refuses such receptivity and thus the "rights" posited by the will can, at best, be only conditional fictions.' I owe this formulation to an anonymous University of Toronto Press reader, to whom I am grateful for the important clarification.
33 George Grant, 'Notebook: Nietzsche Class 1974–5, Book I,' which actually fills two spiral-ring binders. Peter Emberley kindly provided me with a typescript of this notebook.
34 Ibid.
35 Ibid. For texts, Grant chose the works of what he called Nietzsche's third period, 'incomparably the highest, where he looks at the truth and deadliness of science and makes his great affirmations: *Thus Spoke Zarathustra*, his greatest work; *Beyond Good and Evil*, 'which is a commentary on Zarathustra'; and *The Genealogy of Morals*, in which he descended into the popular arena where he must write very directly and exoterically, 'a simpler, more popular, incomparably less ironic [work] than *Beyond Good and Evil*.'
36 Ibid.
37 Ibid.
38 Ibid.
39 Ibid.
40 See *An Introduction to Political Philosophy: Ten Essays by Leo Strauss*, ed. Hilail Gildin (Detroit: Wayne State University Press 1989), 81–98
41 George Grant, 'Notebook: Strauss on Historicism,' [early 1970s?]. However the notebook also contains material on Heidegger's view of Nietzsche, which almost certainly dates from the 1980s.
42 Ibid.
43 Ibid.
44 Ibid.
45 Ibid.
46 George Grant, 'Notebook: Nietzsche Class 1974–5'
47 Ibid.

48 Ibid.
49 George Grant, Notebook: 'Nietzsche Course, Part II, Zarathustra.'
   Grant offered four alternative explanations of its possible meaning:
   1 Although Nietzsche tried to overcome metaphysical dogmatism, he
     unwittingly relapsed into it; or,
   2 Nietzsche proposed the doctrine of the will to power merely as an
     hypothesis, but one that would become true to the extent that it is
     believed and acted upon by human beings; or,
   3 The doctrine of the will to power is superior to all earlier metaphysi-
     cal assertions and is the best possible doctrine for modern human
     beings. However, it is not simply true, because it belongs to a certain
     historical perspective, namely Nietzsche's. Subsequent ages will need
     their own life-affirming perspective; or,
   4 Although the will to power belongs to a specific perspective, this per-
     spective, analogous to Hegel's view of his own philosophy, is the
     absolute perspective.
50 Ibid.
51 Ibid.
52 Ibid.
53 Ibid.
54 Ibid.
55 Ibid.
56 Ibid.
57 Ibid.
58 Ibid.
59 Ibid.
60 Ibid.
61 Ibid.
62 Sheila Grant to William Christian, private communication, 2 June 1994
63 These are the words used by the Anglican Book of Common Prayer to
   refer to the crucifixion.
64 George Grant to Joan O'Donovan, [1982]
65 George Grant, 'Notebook: Nietzsche Course, Part II, Zarathustra'
66 Ibid.
67 Ibid.
68 Ibid.
69 George Grant to Joan O'Donovan, 25 January 1981. Grant did write a
   paper, 'Why Read Rousseau?' but it was never published.

70 Grant always considered Heidegger's work so profound and difficult
that, although he mentioned it often in connection with Nietzsche, it was
only at the time of his death that he was prepared to put his thoughts
down on paper. This essay, 'Confronting Heidegger's Nietzsche,' exists
only in fragmentary form, brilliantly edited and partially completed by
his widow, Sheila Grant. There is no place, even in this lengthy introduction, to begin even a superficial analysis of Grant's thoughts on Hei-
degger-Nietzsche, and I happily leave the task to others much more
qualified than I to undertake it.

71 As he explained to his friend and editor, Dennis Lee: 'I was writing a
book called "Technology and Justice." *English-speaking Justice* was to
be one part; the Nietzsche thing you mention was the national socialist
part and I was working on the marxist part, when I came upon Rousseau
(who I now take to be the founder of the Darwin-Nietzsche part). It was
a great discovery because I realised he was a greater intellectual founder
of modernity than anybody else and it stopped me trying to get down his
greatness and his terrible results. So I have put aside "Technology and
Justice" till I have written the Céline, largely because I was sick of nega-
tivity and criticism and was so enraptured by Céline.' George Grant to
Dennis Lee, November 1983

72 George Grant, 'Nietzsche and the Ancients: Philosophy and Scholarship,'
Dionysius 3 (December 1979): 5–16; rpt. in *Technology and Justice*
(Toronto: House of Anansi 1986), 79–95

73 Ibid., 91

74 Ibid., 92

75 Ibid., 93.

76 Ibid., 94–5

77 George Grant, 'Faith and the Multiversity,' in Grant, *Technology and
Justice*, 35–77. I am particularly concerned here with the discussion that
Grant labels 'Appendix.' Grant began working on this argument in a
paper, 'Christianity and the Modern Multiversity,' delivered at Trinity
College, University of Toronto in 1977.

78 'La foi, c'est l'expérience que l'intelligence est éclairée par l'amour.'
Simone Weil, *La Pesanteur et la Grâce* (Paris: Plon 1948), 148

79 Ibid., 76 See the discussion in William Christian, *George Grant: A Biography* (Toronto: University of Toronto Press 1993), 353–60

80 Ibid., 76

81 George Grant, 'Notebook: Zarathustra,' [1969]

82 Ibid.

83 George Grant, 'Faith and the Multiversity,' 77. The alteration of 'grave-digger' to 'gravediggers' is Sheila Grant's.

84 George Grant, 'Notebook: Zarathustra.' The passage can be found in Hebrews, 10:31.

85 George Grant to Joan O'Donovan, 8 November 1985

Note on the Text

The text of this edition follows the version originally published by CBC Learning Systems as the text of the 1969 CBC Massey Lectures, 'Time as History.' I have supplemented it on occasion with passages transcribed from the broadcast version. These and other minor changes are marked in square brackets. I have also transcribed the sixth program, a dialogue between Grant and the Lebanese diplomat and theologian Charles Malik, which has not been previously published. The chapter titles are those of the broadcast version. They did not appear in the published text. In the Introduction, I have made use of unpublished material from Grant's notebooks. This material will be published eventually as part of the Collected Works of George Grant. Until that time, I hope that the material I have selected for comment will help students and others interested in Grant's view of Nietzsche to understand better how his thought developed from *Time as History* to his later essays 'Nietzsche and the Ancients: Philosophy and Scholarship' and 'Faith and the Multiversity.' The whole text has been copy-edited in University of Toronto Press house style, with minor changes in punctuation, et cetera.

Acknowledgments

Erica Lamacraft was responsible for typing the text of *Time as History*. Mark Haslett of McMaster University provided, as always, help and support. I am grateful to Arthur Davis for his comments on the text and especially for his helpful suggestions regarding the Introduction. I would also like to thank the anonymous University of Toronto Press readers who provided me with comments exemplary in their detail and wisdom. Barbara Christian offered many valuable suggestions that made the Introduction much clearer.

Time as History

To William who taught me to read Nietzsche

1

Time as an Historical Process

[In these talks I am going to discuss the conception of time as history. Next week I will try to enucleate what is being thought when time is conceived as history. What part does such a conception play in what we think ourselves to be? What is its relation to what we think worth doing? After that I will attempt to say something of how this conception came to be in the Western world.

That there is something unique about Western civilization seems to me indubitable when one remembers the fact that in the last three hundred years agents of our civilization have been able to influence, transform, or destroy so many other civilizations. One way of looking at that uniqueness is to look at our conception of time and what enabled the West to bring forth that notion. By looking at the historical origins of that conception I will be thinking within typically modern forms. To think that one understands something chiefly in terms of its historical genesis is itself a fundamental mark of what it is to be modern. Having tried to see what is meant by thinking time as history, I will then connect that symbol to the present crisis in Western civilization, and thereby attempt to make some tentative judgments as to how liberating a symbol this has been for men. In my opinion the thinker who thought the crisis of Western civilization most intensively and most comprehensively was Nietzsche. And often his thought about that crisis was centred about the notions of time and of history. Therefore I will express that crisis by attempting to speak his thought. In the light of these thoughts I will say as best I can what seem to be the advantages and difficulties for men in conceiving time as history.

Let me make two points about method in carrying out this undertaking. One way of making clearer what is assumed about temporality in our civilization is to compare it to what men have thought about time in other civilizations. That human beings can think very differently about such matters is evident if one talks to people from other parts of the world. For example, I live much of my life with people brought up in the Sanskrit culture of India. Just to be with them in the ordinary occurrences of life and death is to be aware of how different is their apprehension of time from my own. Also within differing aspects of the western tradition differences appear. My wife was raised within European Catholicism; I come out of North American liberal Protestantism. To live together is to become aware of how differently time is experienced from within these two sides of Western Christianity.

Of course such differences are more clearly thought by the deepest thinkers of a civilization than by ordinary people. Locke or Rousseau thought the content of their liberalism more explicitly than a practical follower of that faith such as Prime Minister Trudeau has thought them. What is implicitly thought by many who take the presuppositions of their civilization for granted – as granite chunks of faiths – is revealed in its intelligibility by great thinkers who bring out of the granite its form as a statue. Indeed the analogy breaks down because the greatest thinkers may transcend the very granite.

To start from these differences between the conceptions in various civilizations is useful because such comparisons may help us ascend above the particular conceptions of time with which we have been inculcated by our tradition. These days the ascent is especially difficult because the powers of our society for inculcation are very great. Therefore the knowledge of other civilizations is a useful means for making comparisons.

However, comparison between conceptions in different civilizations has danger in it. Its greatest danger is that it may lead to a stultifying relativism. This relativism is asserted by many practitioners of contemporary social science. What is asserted is that different societies are divided from each other by having different absolute presuppositions about the most important matters, for example, What is time?

The presuppositions are absolute because thought at any historical moment is always within them and no man can rise above them to judge between them. I do not think that historicism, so defined, is true and, in making distinctions between conceptions of temporality, I do not want to imply in any way that I am assuming the truth of such historicism. To start from these civilization differences, if not to end with them, is only a possible means of rising to a position in which some perhaps can begin to understand our own conception of time.

The second point is to assert that this discussion should not be thought of as arising simply from the calm of academic retirement. Our conception of time appears to us in the most usual and most intense experiences of our lives in the world. The question is inescapable. How can the dynamic system ever stop expanding? To stop would produce chaos and suffering. It would eliminate those goals in terms of which our civilization defines its life. In speaking of time as history, and in using the general words necessary to its explication, I do not mean to be moving away from what is real for most of us into a formal exercise of specialized vocabulary, but rather to be trying to think what is immediately present for most North Americans in their waking hours – our lives and technological society.]

'History' is one of the key words in which English-speaking people now express what they think they are and what they think the world to be. There are similar words in the other modern Western languages. English, however, is our destiny, and it is now also the destiny of others. In the events of the last two hundred years, English has become the predominant language through which the culture of the Western world expresses itself throughout the globe – whether for good or ill. The polyglot language from that small island off the northwest of Europe is now more than any other the 'lingua franca.' It is well to remember that in speaking our own, we are speaking a world language. And in that language the word 'history' comes forth from lips and pens near the centre of what is most often said. 'History will judge my Vietnam policies,' says a President [Lyndon Johnson]. 'This is a history-making flight,' says an astronaut. 'History' demands, commands, requires, obliges, teaches, etc., etc.

Whatever may be, it is clear that human beings take much of what they are and what their world is through the way that words bring forth that world and themselves to themselves. Other words, such as 'freedom' and 'value,' 'science' and 'nature,' 'personality' and 'attitudes,' are also at the core of what we conceive ourselves to be. But 'history' has particular significance because it is one of those words that is present for us and was not present in any similar sense in the languages of other civilizations – including those from which ours sprang.[1] Therefore if we desire to understand our own understanding of

1 It is often said that our concentration on history comes from our biblical origins. The biblical God of history is compared with the philosophical God of nature. Whatever use there may be in so distinguishing the traditions that come to us from philosophy and from the Bible, it first must be insisted that there are no words in the Bible which should serve as synonyms for what we mean by 'nature' or 'history.'

ourselves, it is well to think about this word, which has come to have such a unique connotation amongst us.

It is not in language in general, but in the words of one collective that the world and ourselves are opened to us. In all groups of languages, for example the European or the Indic, certain languages such as Sanskrit or Greek appear marvellously to transcend limitation, and so have been thought of as called forth for a universal destiny. However, the very liberation through language takes place by the moulding of particular forms. Like food, language not only makes human existence possible, but can also confine it. It is, therefore, useful to think about those parts of our language that particularly express our civilization, and to judge just how these key words have come to determine our apprehensions of what is.

Anybody aware of living in the spearhead of modernity as a North American hears much talk about a crisis in our life. Indeed one manifestation of that crisis is the division between us as to whether the crisis is fundamental. Many of our rulers seem to assume that our way of life may have faults in detail but that basically we are on the right track and that our civilization is the highest ever. On the other hand, significant minorities see what is happening as more than a crisis of detail. Western civilization becomes world-wide just as it becomes increasingly possible for some to doubt its assumptions.

The causes of that doubting cannot be fully described in language that concentrates simply on either outward or inward phenomena. To speak of outward problems, of cities, water and air, poverty, monstrous weapons, and expanding populations, is not sufficient. On the other hand to speak of such inward difficulties as banality in education, alienation from meaning, and widespread nihilism is also not sufficient. Whatever the distinction between outward and inward may mean, our present uncertainties can only be held in our minds by transcending such a extinction. If there be a crisis, it is a crisis about what we are and what we are becoming, both inward and outward. Language itself transcends the distinction between inward and outward. We can hear it and measure it as sound waves; at the same time we know the difference between listening to a foreigner whose speech is meaningless sounds to us, and listening to someone speaking in a language we know and conveying to us intelligible meanings. Like sexuality or religion or music, language transcends the inward-outward distinction.

In this crisis of our present lives in North America, an effort is required to think what we have become. That is manifested to us in language, and central to our language is the word 'history.' To use then the very language that encloses us, it may be said that one of our present historical tasks is to think what we are summing up to ourselves when we use the word 'history.' To touch upon that task is the purpose of the following pages.

'History' is used for many different purposes in our language with shades of differing meaning. There is one division of its use, however, which is more important than any other and which is often a cause of ambiguity. On the one hand the word is used to denote an activity that some men pursue – the study of the past. It is also used to denote a certain kind of reality – human existing – the whole of which, whether in the past, present or future, we call 'history,' and which is distinguished from other kinds of existing. The ambiguity caused by this central division of usage can be seen when we compare the words 'history' and 'biology.' In our educational institutions we study 'life,' not in departments of life, but in departments of biology or in departments of the life sciences. On the other hand, we study history in departments of history, thus using the same word both for the study and what is studied.

Some people like to describe this fact by speaking of the subjective and objective uses of the word 'history'; the subjective being the activity of the studying, the objective being what is studied. This subjective-objective language about the two uses is misleading, because history as a sphere of reality is something in which we take part, and which is therefore only an object for us in the most artificial sense of the word 'objective.' There is indeed an English word ['historiography'] meaning the study of history. In some ways our language would be clearer if we used that word for the study of history, and kept the word 'history' and 'historical' for a special dimension of existence. In fact, we are not going to use the word [historiography] (technical pedantry does not yet entirely determine the development of our language), and therefore the ambiguity of using the same word to describe a dimension of reality and the study of that dimension is going to stay with us. The Germans are coming to make this distinction more clearly in their language by use of two separate words: *Geschichte* for that particular realm of being, historical existence, and *Historie* for the scientific study of the past. Perhaps in English the word history should be kept for the systematic study of the past, while we should find some other word to denote the course of human existence in time. Certainly the Greek original *historia* was used to denote some kinds of human inquiry. [Yet] it is easy to see how the word for inquiry moved in the direction of the study of human affairs. If you wanted to inquire about an event far away in time or space, you went and asked an old person or somebody in another country. Thereby a general word for inquiry came to be used for what had happened in human affairs.

The two uses of the word 'history' – as a study and as an aspect of reality – cannot finally be separated because they are interdependent. We see the enormous interest, [over] the last two hundred years, in the study of man's past from the way that resources have been poured into those studies. Men spend a lifetime understanding the administrative details of earlier empires; a day-to-day description of the literary life of eighteenth-century London is available to us. This would be unlikely outside the belief that knowledge about man will be brought forth by the assiduous study of his genesis and development. Thousands of grown men have believed that they could pene-

trate to the core of the Christian religion by historical studies
about its origins. In other civilizations, men have been quite interested in their past, but never with the passion and hope for
illumination therefrom that have characterized Western historical studies. This is surely because we have believed that man
is essentially an historical being and that therefore the riddle of
what he is may be unfolded in those studies. The thinkers of
other societies have not believed that man was finally understandable as an historical being. Our interest in history as a
study is directly related to our belief that we are historical beings.

It may be argued that [choosing] the word 'history' to distinguish human existence from that of stones and animals is
poor usage, because we now know that birds and stars have a
history as much as men. Two of the great scientific achievements of the nineteenth century were the discovery of the history of the earth in geology and of the development of life in
evolutionary biology. When pre-modern biology, with its doctrine of unchanging species, is compared with modern biology,
which accounts for the origin of the species (how they came to
be and their development through time), one must surely say
that the earth and the beasts have history as much as man.
Indeed in modern thought the idea of history is everywhere.
Not only men and stones and animals have history, but
philosophers such as Whitehead write as if God has a biography.
Even reason, which was traditionally conceived as transcending all development, has been given its own history. The most
beautiful modern book on the subject, Kant's *Critique of Pure
Reason*, ends with a section on the history of pure reason.[2]
The modern concentration on man as historical is but an aspect

2 This section of Kant's first *Critique* has generally been neglected by English-
speaking commentators. Indeed the British have in their commentaries on
Kant generally tried to turn that genius into one of their own. To put the
matter simply, they neglect the fact that Kant paid an even greater tribute
to Rousseau than he did to Hume.

of a whole way of conceiving temporality, which, it is claimed, allows us to understand more adequately the story not only of our own species, but of everything. In such a usage, the account of man's collective development through the ages is held together with the development of other beings, for example, the beasts evolving and the earth coming to be through millennia. The word 'history' does not mean a particular kind of reality, because it is used about all forms of reality. It is what we must know about something to understand that something. To know about anything is to know its genesis, its development up to the present, and as much of its future as we can. Perhaps it may be said that the greatest difference be-tween the ancient and modern accounts of knowledge is this modern concentration on the genesis of something in order to know it. History (call it, if you will 'process') is that to which all is subject, including our knowing, including God, if we still find reasons for using that word.

Yet as soon as this is said we must see that within the modern project the human is at other times clearly distinguished from the non-human, and the word 'history' appropriated for this distinction. 'History' is distinguished from 'nature.' The modern physics of Galileo, Descartes, and Newton accounted for the 'physical' world (including our own bodies) as understandable in terms of mechanics, and without final cause. But immediately, questions about men arose for those who so conceived nature: how men, who are part of such a nature, have still the freedom to know it, and even more, how their determination by this nature affects their freedom to do good or evil. Those thinkers who were unwilling to reduce what they considered the undoubted 'given' of morality, and at the same time accepted the new account of nature, reconciled any difficulty in so doing by showing forth our lives as lived in two realms – that of nature and that of freedom. It was indeed in this intellectual crisis (the attempt to understand the modern scientific conception of nature that excluded any idea of final

purpose, and to relate that conception to human purposive-
ness) that the modern conception of history first made its
appearance in the thought of men such as Rousseau, Kant, and
Hegel. The realm of history was distinguished from the realm
of nature. 'History' was used to describe the particular human
situation in which we are not only made but make. In this way
of speaking, history was not a term to be applied to the development of the earth and animals, but a term to distinguish the
collective life of man (that unique being who is subject to
cause and effect as defined in modern science, but also a member of the world of freedom).

As a North American, living outside Europeanness, and yet
inheriting from many sides of the European tradition, it is perhaps worth stating that by and large it has been the English
thinkers who have insisted that we apply the word 'history' to
stones and birds as well as to man, while it has been the German and French thinkers who have insisted on the unique
human situation, and who have used the distinction between
nature and history to make that clear. To them, man alone should
be called essentially historical, because he not only suffers
history, but in freedom can make it.

Both these ways of looking at man and the world are but
facets of modernity. Indeed these two languages are used together in the sermons preached by our journalists about the
achievement of landing on the moon. These events are called
another upward step in the march of evolution, one of the
countless steps since life came out of the sea. Man and nature
are seen together. On the other hand, in the same sermons there
is talk of man in his freedom conquering nature, indeed transcending himself. In as archetypal an event for technological
man as the space program, it is right that the two languages
should come together in the hymning of the achievement. The
two languages come together as man is seen not only as a part
of evolution, but as its spearhead who can consciously direct
the very process from which he came forth. In such speaking,

man is either conceived as the creator, who arose from an accidental evolution, or if evolution is itself conceived within a terminology about the divine, man is then viewed as a co-operator, a co-creator with God. This latter language is presently very popular in the United States, particularly among those who want to include Christian or Jewish theology within the liberal ideology of their society.

However these two sides of the modern project may be put together, my purpose is to write about the word history as it is used about existence in time, not as it is used to describe a particular academic study. I am not concerned with historical inquiry, its proper purposes and methods, to what extent it is a science and if a science, how it differs from physics or mathematics, to what extent we can have correct knowledge of the past, etc., etc. These are technical questions for those who earn their living by being historians, or philosophers of [historiography], and want to think about how best to practise their profession. All such professions, be they practical arts or theoretical sciences or a mixture of both – physicists, historians, dentists – have their own trade papers in which the methods of their particular occupation are discussed. Such occupational matters are not my business. I am concerned with what it means to conceive the world as an historical process, to conceive time as history and man as an historical being.

Words such as 'time' arise from the fact that existing is a coming to be and a passing away. Our doing and our making (perhaps even our thinking) occur within time's thrall. Because 'has been,' 'is now,' and 'will be' make possible our purposes but also dirempt us of them, it is no wonder that through the ages men have tried to understand the temporality of their lives. In our age, astonishment about that temporality has been calmed by apprehending it above all as history. It is this conception of time as history that I wish to try to enucleate.

To enucleate means to extract the kernel of a nut, the seed of a tree. In the present case, there appears around us and in us the presence that Western men have made – modern technical society. It has been made by men who did what they did out of a vision of what was important to do. In that vision is the conception of time as history. The word 'enucleation' implies that I am not simply interested in describing the manifestations of that vision, for example the mastery of movement through space or the control of heredity. Rather I try to partake in the seed from which the tree of manifestations has come forth. But the metaphor fails because to extract a kernel may be to expose it as a dead thing rather than as a potential tree. In another age, it would have been proper to say that I am attempting to partake in the soul of modernity. When we are intimate with another person we say that we know him. We mean that we partake, however dimly, in some central source from which proceeds all that the other person does or thinks or feels. In that partaking even his casual gestures are recognized. That source was once described as the character of his soul. But modern knowing, in a strict sense, has excluded the conception of the soul as a superstition, inimical to scientific exactness. To know about human beings is to know about their behaviour and to be able to predict therefrom. But it is not about the multiform predictable behaviours of modern technical society that I wish to write. It is about the animating source from which those behaviours come forth.

What I am not doing is what is done by modern behavioural social science, which is not interested in essences. A leading behavioural political scientist, Mr David Easton, said recently: 'We could not have expected the Vietnam War.' This was said by a man whose profession was to think about political behaviour in North America, and whose methods were widely accepted by other scientists. But not to have expected the Vietnam War was not to have known that the chief political animation of the United States is that it is an empire. My use of the word enucleate indicates that I do not wish to use a method that cannot grasp such animations.

To write of the conception of time as history and to think of it as an animator of our existence is not, however, to turn away from what is immediately present to all of us. When I drive on the highways around Hamilton and Toronto, through the proliferating factories and apartments, the research establishments and supermarkets; when I sit in the bureaucracies in which the education for technocracy is planned; when I live in and with the mechanized bodies and resolute wills necessary to that system; it is then that the conception of time as history is seen in its blossoming. An animating vision is not known simply in a retired academic thinking, but in the urgent experience of every lived moment. The words used to explicate 'time as history' may seem abstract, but they are meant to illuminate our waking and sleeping hours in technical society.

2
Temporality and Technological Man

Those who study history are concerned with the occurrences of passed times; those who conceive time as history are turned to what will happen in the future. When we speak of the present historical situation we are oriented to the future, in the sense that we are trying to gather together the intricacies of the present so that we can calculate what we must be resolute in doing to bring about the future we desire. The accomplishments of modern society are every year more before us, not simply as they once were as hoped for dreams, but as pressing realizations. The magnitude of those modern accomplishments, as compared with those of other civilizations, lies in what they enable us to do by our mastery through prediction over human and non-human nature. These accomplishments were the work of men who were determined to make the future different from what the past had been, men oriented to that future in which greater events than have yet been, will be. They conceived time as that in which human accomplishments would be unfolded; that is, in the language of their ideology, as progress. Whatever differences there may have been between the three dominant ideologies of our century – marxist communism, American liberalism, national socialism –

they all similarly called men to be resolute in their mastery of the future. Four centuries ago, those who thought of mastering the future were a dreaming minority, forced to work subtly against those with some other account of time. Today such men are our unquestioned rulers, welcomed by the overwhelming majority in both East and West. To enucleate the conception of time as history must then be to think our orientation to the future together with the will to mastery. Indeed the relation between mastery and concentration on the future is apparent in our language. The word will is used as an auxiliary for the future tense, and also as the word that expresses our determination to do.

Men have always attempted to understand what is meant by the future and what knowledge or control we can have of it. Certainly we must make the limited statement that a future awaits, and in that sense is an inescapable presence for us. When young we must be turned to the future for the realization of our potentialities, and we are aware of the future even as it becomes slowly clear that eventually and inevitably there will be no future for us as individuals. We die in the knowledge that tomorrow's dawn will not be present for us. We may be so egocentric that in that dying we hardly care about its coming for others. But can we reach that pitch of solipsism in which we are able to think that our death is the end of the world? In these atomic days the end of the race as a whole can easily be imagined; but imagining includes the sun rising over a humanless planet. Whatever certain modern philosophers have meant by the mind making the object, they did not mean that we could deny a future in our imagining. Whatever the physicists may mean in showing us the increasing randomness of the elementary things, they are not asking us to think what it would be for nothing to be happening. Some theologians have conceived time as a creature. But to use that language sensibly (that is, not as some extension from human making to explain our dependence upon God) it must be recognized that the language of creation leaves us always with the question: what does it mean to speak of the end of time? – certainly not, after time. The word creativity is only properly used about God and not about man. It is an abyss in which the human mind is swallowed up, and those of us who use it must recognize it as such a limit. It is not possible to imagine what it would be for nothing (or better for no event) to be occurring. To speak of the future as potential and not actual does not deny its presence for us. Those of our contemporaries who, in their revolt against the doctrine of progress and its concentration on living for the future, assert that living is always in the present are saying something North Americans need to hear. But they distort the truth about time, if in so saying they assume that the future is not with us, although in a less articulated presentation.

Yet that which is there for us potentially can only be there in an undetailed way. In the public world, who would have guessed in the early 1960s that the Kennedy dynasty would move into the 1970s with an uncertain political future, while Mr Nixon would be in the seat of political authority?

To deny all chance in the name of a predicting science may be logically possible but the nearer we get to the details of life, the more clearly it invalidates common sense. Yet the inscrutability and unpredictability of events must not be over-emphasized, in either the individual or the collective case. We can plan our lives so that within limits the future depends on what we have done and are doing. This is truer collectively than individually because of the greater ability of the collective to control the results of chance. The success of the planned moon landing did not fluctuate because of the assassination of the president who had made the decision that it was to be an imperial purpose. (Indeed the greater ability of collective than of individual purposes to be sustained against accidents is one of the reasons why, in an age given over to making the future, we all more and more truly exist in the collective, and less and less pursue purposes that transcend it.) Indeed our surrender to the oil cartels has taught us ecologically that the 'best laid schemes o' mice an' men gang aft a-gley.' It would be, however, facile pessimism to carry the tag too far. Human purposive doing is both possible and potent. And the more complex that which we wish to accomplish, the more we have to envisage the future in which it will be accomplished.

The presence of the future in our imagining is one reason why men are so effective in their doing. It is not necessary to be able to define satisfactorily the difference between men and the other animals to recognize that human beings are able to accomplish more purposes than the members of other species. Both men and the other animals are in an environment in which their food and their shelter, their protection and their continuance, are not given to them without organization. They have to take continuing steps in arranging and using other parts of nature so that these ends can be achieved. (By way of parenthesis I would say that, in the past at least, those nations and classes within nations [that] have come through generations of ease to take their food, shelter, and protection for granted, as given in the nature of things, have not long survived. Some now hope that this is no longer the case.) But men are so much more potent and therefore so much more violent than other animals in this using and arranging. Other species also have histories – for example, certain birds changed their migrations after the glacial age. But human beings have more history because they are capable of more differentiated doing, and this capability depends upon openness to an imagined future and the power to plan towards that future. Whatever is the correct use of the word 'novelty,' we can bring more novelty into the future than any other species. To deny novelty may be to speak in some true way that moderns cannot penetrate, but it is at least contradicted in common sense understanding, by many human projects.

The more we are concentrated on the future as the most fascinating reality, the more we become concentrated on that side of our existence that is concerned with making happen. The more we can make happen novel events that come forth in the potential future, the more properly can we be called historical beings. When we single out somebody as an historical individual, or a people as an historical people, we surely mean that those in question have been in their doing the makers of events. Thus the English were an historical people in harnessing new power to industry, and in beating their European rivals in taking it around the world. In our generation Chairman Mao is an historical individual in bringing European technology to the Chinese masses, by uniting Chinese and European politics. In this sense we can say that just as men are more historical than other animals, so in the last centuries Western men have been more historical than the other civilizations still present, and than those civilizations we superseded geographically. Ours has been a dynamic civilization and that dynamism has been related to the fact that our apprehension of temporality was concentrated on the future. 'Has been' and 'is now' weakened in our consciousness compared with 'will be.' The concentration upon time as future and the dynamism of doing fed upon each other. As Westerners found their hope in an imaginable future, they turned more and more to mastery; their concentration on mastery eliminated from their minds any partaking in time other than as future. Equally, the clarification of this conception of time by thinkers and the intensified making of novelty by practical men were mutually interdependent. As Europeans achieved more and more mastery through their works, thinkers increasingly defined time as history. As words such as 'progress' and 'history' were placed in the centre of the most comprehensive thought, so practical men were encouraged thereby to justify their conquests as the crown of human activity. Also (as I have tried to describe elsewhere), we North Americans whose ancestors crossed the ocean were, because of our religious traditions and because this continent was experienced as pure potentiality (a *tabula rasa*), the people most exclusively enfolded in the conception of time as progress and the exaltation of doing that went with it.[1] We were to be the people who, after dominating two European wars, would become the chief leaders in establishing the reign of technique throughout all the planet and perhaps beyond it.

The accomplishments of masterful doing lead us to think about the language of willing. When we say that somebody has a strong will we mean that there is a resoluteness through time about his determination to carry out his purposes in the world. It says little about how much he may have deliberated about those purposes, nothing about their nobility. To state the obvious: in a university one knows many thoughtful people, irresolute in decision; in the political world one meets decisive men whose purposes are little deliberated. For example, in the regime of the Kennedys there was much rhetoric about decisiveness, but we may well ask (in the light of the results of their decisions, for example, towards South East Asia or towards De Gaulle) whether there was sufficient deliberation on what it was important to be decisive about. The language surrounding the word 'will' summons up human doing and distinguishes it from our thinking or feeling. I do not wish here to give a justification of what is currently described and abused as faculty psychology: the doctrine that speaks of a power of human beings to will, to think, to suffer, etc. We need, however, some language that catches the determination necessary to our doings, and distinguishes that from our other activities. When Shakespeare writes of the Macbeths' determination to be rulers, he puts into Lady Macbeth's mouth the following words to her husband at their decisive moment: 'But screw your courage to the sticking-place, and we'll not fail.' What is required of them is not further thought about their desire to rule, nor further calculation about the means to that end, but

1 See Grant, *Technology and Empire* (House of Anansi: Toronto 1969).

an unflinching 'will' to carry out the deeds that she believes will realize what they want.

The language of will that summons forth for us the deeds of men is found in many civilizations – not only among people who conceive time as history. But the language of willing has been at the very core of Western men's account of themselves. However, the reference of that language is often uncertain. Some have used it as if willing were simply a kind of thinking; others as if it were desiring. Neither seems to me satisfactory. Therefore, to approach the language of 'willing' it is useful to relate it to our 'desiring' and 'thinking' and then to distinguish it therefrom.

What we are determined to do is clearly related to our thought about purposes and our calculating about the means to those purposes. But however long and beautifully men deliberate about purposes, however carefully they calculate, there comes the moment when they either bring about or do not bring about certain events. Willing is that power of determining by which we put our stamp on events (including ourselves) and in which we do some violence to the world. In willing to do or not to do we close down on the openness of deliberation and decide that as far as we are concerned, this will happen rather than that. Indeed, one strange ambiguity among human beings is that what seems required for the greatest thought is opposite to what is required for the greatest doing. If our thinking is not to be procrustean, we require an uncertain and continuous openness to all that is; certainty in closing down issues by decision is necessary for great deeds. In thought about the most important matters there is nothing we need do, there is nothing we can wish to change.

It is more difficult to distinguish the language of willing from desiring, particularly because of the history of the English language. Indeed from the changes in the use of the word 'will' can be seen the changes in what men thought they were. In its beginnings the word 'will' is most often used synonymously with wishing or wanting or desiring, and yet also it is used in the sense of determining or making happen.[2] When we use the erotic language of wanting or desiring, we express our dependence on that which we need – be it food, another person, or God. The language of desire is always the language of dependence. Some English uses of 'willing' are closely identified with this language of need. Yet as we enter the modern era the language of will comes more and more to be used about making happen what happens. Here it becomes the assertion of the power of the self over something other than the self, and indeed of the self over its own dependencies. The dependence of desire passes over into the mastery. In related language, Kant, who always so brilliantly expressed what it is to be a modern as against a classical man, made the modern use clear when he maintained that we cannot will a purpose without willing means to bring it about. 'To wish' or 'to want' can be casual when we are not serious about what happens in the world; 'to will' means that we are serious about actualizing our purposes. To will is to legislate; it makes something positive happen or prevents something from happening. Willing is then the expression of the responsible and independent self, distinguished from the dependent self who desires.

Indeed as soon as we look at the modern era, we see how the language of willing has taken on a significance not present in other civilizations. On Marx's tomb at Highgate in London is inscribed his most famous aphorism: 'The philosophers have only interpreted the world in various ways. The point however is to change it.'[3] Here we are called to master the world through

---

2 The philological question is complicated by the fact that the word 'will' has its origin in two distinct old English verbs 'willan' and 'willian.' It is therefore difficult to follow the development of its use.

3 It is interesting for Canadians that Marx's tomb is close to Lord Strathcona's – the man who more than any other was responsible for the actual building of the CPR, a noble deed making possible the possibility of Canada.

our doing and to make it as we want it. Greek heroes were summoned to be resolute for noble doing, but their deeds were not thought of as changing the very structure of what is, but as done rather for the sake of bringing into immediacy the beauty of a trusted order, always there to be appropriated through whatever perils. In the modern call, human wills are summoned to a much more staggering challenge. It is our destiny to bring about something novel; to conquer an indifferent nature and make it good for us. Indeed in that summons our wills come to be thought of as operating within a quite different context. Human willing is no longer one type of agent in a total process of natural agents, all of which are directed towards the realization of good purposes. We now see our wills as standing above the other beings of nature, able to make these other beings serve the purposes of our freedom. All else in nature is indifferent to good. Our wills alone are able, through doing, to actualize moral good in the indifferent world. It is here that history as a dimension of reality, distinguished from nature, comes to be thought. History is that dimension in which men in their freedom have tried to 'create' greater and greater goodness in the morally indifferent world they inhabit. As we actualize meaning, we bring forth a world in which living will be known to be good for all, not simply in a general sense, but it the very details we will be able more and more to control. Time is a developing history of meaning that we make. The self-conscious animal has always been plagued by anxiety as to whether it is good to be in the world. But to modern man, though life may not yet be meaningful for every one, the challenge is to make it so. Upon our will to do has been placed the whole burden of meaning.

To distinguish the language of willing and thinking, and then to say that modern life has near its centre the will's challenge to itself to make the world, must in no way imply that the modern world is not made by reasoning. Such an implication would be absurd because it would disregard the chief mark of the modern era – the progress of the sciences. The systematic use of reasoning and experimenting in order to know objectively – that is, for knowledge to be accumulated collectively by the race through the generations – has been and is increasingly the central achievement of our civilization. Indeed the idea of time as history was more shaped in response to the progressive sciences than by anything else. In the methodology by which the scientists of the last centuries carried out their activities, the race had at last found the sure and certain path that would guarantee that knowledge would increase among men, collectively. The belief in progress gained its power over the minds of intelligent men through this recognition, more than through anything else. The will to change the world was a will to change it through the expansion of knowledge.

This is how willing and reasoning have come together in the modern era. At a superficial level it is obvious that the ability of men to discover how the world works can be used to improve the conditions of man's estate. This relation between the discoveries of science and their use for human good has been the cause of the great public respect for the scientist. But leaving the matter there might imply that the modern relation between willing and reasoning is an external one, in which practical men simply turn into technology what the scientists happen to discover. Such a conception leads to the false view that the relation between technology and science is an external, not an intrinsic one. It leads to that popular falsehood, namely that scientists just find out what their pure curiosity leads them to, and that it is up to society to decide whether that knowledge be used for good or ill. Such statements must be denied, not because they might free scientists from responsibility for the results of their discoveries, but because they imply a false description of what scientists do.

The coming together of willing and reasoning lies essentially in the method that has made possible the successes of modern science. The world is a field of objects that can be known in their workings through the 'creative' acts of reasoning and experimenting by the thinking subject who stands over them. This brings together willing and reasoning, because the very act of the thinking-ego standing over the world, and representing it to himself as objects, is a stance of the will. This statement could only be substantiated by a careful analysis of the work of the greatest modern scientists and philosophers, [that is,] how they illuminated what they were doing in their science. It would require thinking through what they meant by such words as 'object' and 'subject,' 'representation' and 'experiment,' what the word 'technique' has come to mean for us, and above all what is now meant by 'mathematics.'[4] I have not the time to do that here nor indeed the capability. But in turning from this question, I leave incomplete the enucleation of what we are thinking when we think time as history. However, as the methods of modern science are more and more applied to understanding human beings, in what are now called 'the social sciences,' it becomes easier to grasp what is meant by our science being a kind of willing, because in the social sciences the stance of the subject-scientist standing over against the object-society has very immediate and pressing consequences for us, since we are the objects.

When Marx wrote of changing the world, he still believed that changing was not an end in itself, but the means to a future society conducive to the good life for all. Overcoming the chances of an indifferent nature by technique and politics was an interim stage until conditions should be ripe for the realization of men's potential goodness. For all his denial of past thought, he retained from that past the central truth about human beings – namely, that there is in man a given humanness that it is our purpose to fulfil. So equally in the sentimentalized marxism of Marcuse, the victory of the will over nature is not an end in itself, but simply a means to that time when

4 This has been thought most illuminatingly by Heidegger.

men will find happiness in the polymorphous liberation of their instincts. The burden on the will to make the meaning of the world is thus limited by the belief that in some unspecified future the age of willing will be at an end. Even the traditional capitalist ideologists, who believed that changing the world was best achieved by sanctifying greed, had some vision of the fulfilled state of man (albeit a vulgar one) that transcended changing the world.

In the conceptions of history now prevalent among those 'creative' men who plan the mastery of the planet, changing the world becomes ever more an end in itself. It is undertaken less simply to overcome the natural accidents that frustrate our humanity and more and more for the sheer sake of the 'creation' of novelty. This movement inevitably grows among the resolute as the remnants of any belief in a lovable actuality disappear. We will, not so much for some end beyond will, but for the sake of the willing itself. In this sense, the challenge of the will is endless to the resolute, because there is always more 'creation' to be carried out. Our freedom can even start to make over our own species.

As Hegel so clearly expounded, doing is in some sense always negation. It is the determination that what is present shall not be; some other state shall. But it is positive in the sense that in its negating of what is, it strives to bring forth its own novel 'creations.' In this sense the burden of creation itself is placed upon us. Resoluteness for that task becomes the key virtue for the history makers – a resoluteness that finds the sources of novelty in their own 'values.' They assert that meaning is not found in what is actually now present for us, but in that which we can yet bring to be.

3
Nietzsche and Time as History

[In our period the world that has been brought into existence by those who have conceived time as history begins to reach its apogee. Those who have dreamed since Machiavelli of controlling the planet by technology are no longer a minority working subtly against those with some other vision, but have become our unquestioned rulers, loved by the overwhelming majority. The achievements of the modern conception are all before us, not as some hoped-for dream, but in their realization. Do I have to list them? Its disasters are equally before us. Do I have to list *them* (too)? As these realizations are so pressingly manifest, the nature of the conception presents itself unavoidably as a question to be unfolded.]

An obvious question is why the conception of time as history came to its flowering in the West, rather than in one of the other great civilizations. Why have Western men come to think as they think and do as they do? Why was it our destiny to raise up 'willing' and 'orientation to the future' so that they have become universal ways of men's existing? As in the most hidden aspects of our lives we cannot come to know ourselves without recognizing our own familial histories, in all their idiosyncracy, so equally we cannot come to know ourselves with-

out recognizing how our enfolding civilization came to be what
it is. Such a search for recognition must start from the truism
that the two chief sources of modern 'Westernness' are the Bible
and the relics of Greek civilization. However, care must be
taken that this truism is not turned into the idea that the origins
of our 'rationality' are Greek, while we receive our 'religion'
from the Bible. This is a distortion of our origins, because both
among the Greeks and in the Bible thought and reverence are
sustained together. Also as these origins came out into the West
they were held together in ways 'too deep, too numerous, too
obscure, even simply too beautiful for any ease of intellectual
relation.' Many of the deepest controversies in which Western
men have defined what they are have been centred around the
proper ways of relating or distinguishing what was given to
them from Athens and Jerusalem.

If we were searching for the origins of our present, we
would first try to state what was given to men in Judaism or
Christianity, and then seek out how this intermingled with the
claims of universal understanding which were found in the
heights of Greek civilization. As Christianity was the majori-
tarian locus in which that intermingling occurred, we would
have to examine how it was that Christianity so opened men
to a particular consciousness of time, by opening them to anxiety and charity; how willing was exalted through the stamp-
ing proclamations of the creating Will; how time was raised up
by redemption in time, and the future by the exaltation of the
eschaton. But to recognize ourselves today, we cannot turn simply to our origins in Athens and Jerusalem, because those *aitiai*[1]
are obscured for us by the massive criticism which the thinkers
and scientists and scholars have carried on for the last centuries. That criticism so penetrates every part of our education
that we cannot hope to reach back easily to make these origins
present. Indeed even that penetrating criticism – which scholars

1 Grant wrote *aitia*. He is using the Greek work in the sense of 'causes.' *Ed.*

hypostatize as the Enlightenment – is itself ambiguous insofar as it is penetrated by an acceptance of certain aspects of that which was being criticized. This is just the truism that the modern conception of progress may be characterized as secular Christianity. As in the relations of children and parents, the conception of time as history in its first optimistic and liberal formulation was at one and the same time a critical turning away from our origins and also a carrying along of some essential aspects of them. Even today as the liberal formulation of time as history disappears before the hammer blows of the twentieth century, we are left with a more frightening conception of time as history which holds within it that presence of anxiety and willing which came from our particular origins.

[Unless we know that we carry with us the long shaping of what our ancestors have been, how can we know what we are now? The alternative method would be to turn to what is here now and what in that is potentiality for the future. For example, I could take the fact that we move fast to the point where man may be able to make man. The signs grow that we approach the point when the traditional but chancy method of intercourse between the sexes (however dear it may be) may no longer be the chief means whereby which we perpetuate our species. Our control over nature moves to the moment when we may be able to perpetuate the species by more rational means. When we try to think what these means are, when we try to think what are and what are not their potentialities, we are led to think what we mean by our freedom, what we mean by nature, indeed what we mean by time as history.

Both these alternative methods of looking at the conception – either by understanding it through its genesis, or by bringing forth the potentialities of its present – are necessary to understanding it. Yet how do we hold these two methods together? If either is taken separately, it falls into a particular danger. If we turn to the past, and understand the conception in its genesis, we can easily find ourselves impotent and irrelevant for living in the full reality of the present. Just go into the arts faculty of a university. Never has a society put such resources into scholarship about the past as has ours in North America. Yet never has there been a society where what is known about the past is so irrelevant to our living.

One bad result of turning to the past may be that men are left with such a sense of ambiguity that they are unable to consider any relevance that past has now for present living, and so are made impotent. They are submerged by the sheer relativity they find in history. Indeed some can look to scholarship about the past as a sanctuary from the present. They find in study a means of pretending they do not live in the twentieth century. So much of our modern education in humanities first makes students impotent by drumming into them the sheer relativism to be derived from the past, and then training them to fit into the sanctuary of objective scholarship. One of the brightest possibilities in contemporary student unrest is their revolt against the irrelevance of modern scholarship, and the way it hides its meaninglessness under the rhetoric of objectivity.

On the other hand, if we turn to the present to understand its potentialities, we are easily led into the opposite danger. We tend to comprehend the present only within its own terms. At its worst this turns science into calculating how we can use that present for our most immediate purposes. Scientists advise governments on juvenile delinquency, taxation policy, urban renewal, defoliation in Vietnam. The danger of immediacy is also present in many of the radical students who, in reaction against the service of the multiversity to the imperial interests, propose that all thought in the universities be made relevant to reform or revolt. This tends to as great an immediacy as that of the scientific bureaucrats the radicals despise.

Of course in both cases some of the resulting activity is good, some wicked and much pointless. But what must be said in the present connection is that such immediacy can only be a stance for calculating, not for thinking the modern. To look at

what we are in our present realization of time as history, it is
necessary on the one hand to avoid a scholarship that by its
immersion in the past castrates our thinking about what it is to
exist now, and on the other hand to avoid an immediacy that
trivializes by persuading us that we are understanding the
modern when in fact we are being carried along by the waves
of its dynamism.

Only the greatest thinkers transcend scholarship without
preaching easy acceptance of shallow activism.] However, it
is not possible in lectures such as these to sort out the com-
plexity of the geneses of what we now are. Therefore I turn
away from a search for the fundamentals of the Western past
to the thoughts of that writer where the conception of time as
history is most luminously articulated.

Nearly a hundred years ago Nietzsche thought the conception of time as history more comprehensively than any other
modern thinker before or since. He did not turn away from
what he thought. That is, for good or ill, he accepted 'en pleine
conscience de cause' that temporality enfolds human beings
and that they experience that temporality as history. Yet he
also understood, better than any other thinker, the profundity
of the crisis that such a recognition must mean for those who
have accepted it. Therefore in trying to follow Nietzsche's
thought, we can go further in thinking what it means to conceive that time is history. Moreover, in looking at the flowering
tree at the height of its wildest blooming, we are not far from
its seed and its seed bed.

There are certain difficulties which stand in the way of
English-speaking people listening seriously to Nietzsche. The
cataclysms of violence which have occurred between the English-
speaking peoples and the Germans, in this century, make it
hard for us to look at the German tradition without suspicion.
Many English-speaking intellectuals write about Nietzsche in
the tone of personal discrediting. This often has the mark of
those who wish to inoculate themselves against thoughts they do

not want to think by calumniating the author of those thoughts. Although we can exclude by such inoculation the thought of Nietzsche explicitly from our minds, we are still caught in its implicit presence. For example, modern sociology is central to our North American way of living. The chief founder of that sociology was Max Weber. And certainly Weber's sociology must be taken, more than anything else, as a commentary on his engrossed encounter with Nietzsche's writings.

In much writing in English, Nietzsche is spoken of as a second-rate poet masquerading as a philosopher, or as an aphorist who did not face questions comprehensively, or as a romantic of the feelings who was not concerned with science. His thoughts are impugned by the fact that he retreated into madness (to use that ambiguous word). In the worst condemnation he is accused of being a fountainhead of National Socialism and open to what is called today anti-Semitism. (Anti-Judaism is a more accurate name for that baseness.)

To start from the worst of these accusations, Nietzsche's works are filled with his loathing of anti-Judaism and of his understanding of its particular danger in certain German circles. He clearly would have been disgusted by the Nazis, that union of a desperate ruling class, of romantic nationalism among the bourgeoisie, and the industrial gutter. As for romanticism, his deepest book is indeed in dramatic form a conscious parody of the New Testament, which sometimes breaks into poetic utterance. But his other writings are in limpid prose which expounds difficult philosophic questions with breathtaking clarity. This picture of Nietzsche as a second-rate romantic poet was partly created among the English by the absurd early translations of his work. His German was translated onto a phoney Gothic English, filled with words such as 'thou' and 'spake.' Above all, this obscured Nietzsche's great wit with a patina of pretentiousness. In fact, there are few works of modern comedy which could rank beside *The Case of Wagner*. As for modern science, nobody ever more emphasized its achievements, took these achievements to be the centre of the modern world, and pondered on the nature of that science. It shows a good understanding of the course of modern science to predict in the 1870s: 'The dynamic interpretation of the world will shortly gain power over the physicists.' He was, at 24, a professor of philology at a great European university. It is indeed true that he spent the last years of his life in madness. One must remember, however, that he was the first thinker to bring out the very great difference in the use of the word 'madness' in modern thought as compared to the traditional meaning of that term.

At a deeper level, I must say that in using the thought of Nietzsche to enucleate the conception of time as history, I in no sense imply that what he said is the best or highest word about what is. Nor do I imply that however much he would have loathed the Nazis, he is free from any responsibility for their power in Germany. The very clarity and force of his criticism of the European past liberated many Germans from the traditional religious and moral restraints of their tradition, so that they were opened to a barren nihilism which was a fertile field for the extremities and absurdities of National Socialism. Nor do I imply that his lucid but immoderate rhetoric is the best way to put forth one's thoughts. Indeed it might have been better for humanity if Nietzsche's works of high genius had never been written, or if written, published. But to raise this possibility implies that it is better, at least for most men, not to be told where they are. Nietzsche's words raise to an intensely full light of explicitness what it is to live in this era. He articulates what it is to have inherited existence as a present member of Western history. His thought does not invent the situation of our contemporary existing; it unfolds it. He carries the crisis of modern thought further only in the sense that by the accuracy and explicitness of his unfolding, he makes it more possible for others to understand the situation of which they are the inheritors. But the inheritance of modern Western man was something that Nietzsche took over as a given fate from what others had done and thought, made and felt before him. He made explicit what had been implicit. Therefore, to say that it would have been better for Nietzsche's words not to have been published implies that some men can live better if they know less where they are. From whom should some knowledge be hidden? How much is it good for any one person to know?

I raise this question to make clear that I do not intend to take up Nietzsche's words as journalists take up the thoughts of others on television. They call thoughts fascinating and controversial, and in so doing castrate them for themselves and for their audience by cutting off those thoughts from any connection with actuality. The work is done through the implication that no thought can rise above the level of opinion, and therefore be something more important than a source of entertainment. I would not want to trivialize Nietzsche, as if I wished to entertain the bored with a 'controversial' figure. To speak about his thoughts on history implies that as the present situation is what it is in any case, it is better to know that situation for what it is, than to live in it without so knowing. Whether this is a correct judgment depends on a difficult argument in political philosophy.

Indeed some of what Nietzsche says will seem obvious today, so that the response may easily be: 'What's so new?' In the century since he began to write, not only have his opinions filtered down unrecognized through lesser minds to become the popular platitudes of the age, but also what he prophesied is now all around us to be easily seen. Nevertheless, though his more obvious teachings have become the platitudes of such schools as positivism and existentialism, psychiatry and behavioural social science, the subtler consequences of extremity he draws necessarily from them are not much contemplated. Most men want it both ways in thought and in practice; the nobility of Nietzsche is that he did not.

In *Human, All Too Human* Nietzsche says: 'Lack of historical sense is the inherited defect of all philosophers.' Or again:
'What separates us from Kant, as from Plato and Leibnitz, is
that we believe that becoming is the rule even in the spiritual
things. We are historians from top to bottom ... They all to a
man think unhistorically, as is the age-old custom among
philosophers.' Previous philosophers have taken their contemporaries as if they were man as he always is, and proceeded
from their definition of that supposedly unchanging being to
make generalizations about the meaning of human life, and
even about the whole of which man is a part. But it has become evident that all species, human as much as non-human,
can only be understood as continually changing, that is, as
having histories. Darwin made this patently clear about the
other animals. There are not types of animals that are always
on earth; species come to be, are in continual change and pass
away. The same is so about ourselves. What is fundamental
about all human behaviour (including our understanding of it
– itself a behaviour) is its historicity.

To repeat, this does not seem very new today. Every liter-
ate high school student would take a simple statement of this
historicism for granted. We are taught early to use the language of values, to say that our values are dependent on our
historical situation and that this generalization proceeds from
any objective study of the past. Civilizations and individuals
have lived by different values. As there is no way of judging
between the value of these values, we are taught early a very
simple historical relativism. As we go farther in our education, we are taught to express that historicism with greater
sophistication. However, the almost universal acceptance of
this relativism by even the semi-literate in our society is very
recent. The belief that men are enfolded in their historicity,
and the consequent historical relativism with its use of the
word 'values,' only began to be the popular vocabulary in this
century.

Nietzsche is the first thinker who shows how this historicity is to be recognized in the full light of its consequences, in every realm of existence. To repeat, most previous philosophers have shown their lack of historical sense by trying to insist, in some form or other, that there is something permanent in human beings, individually or collectively, which survives through change and in terms of which we can be defined. From that definition can be drawn out a scale of better and worse purposes for ourselves and others. But as Nietzsche says in *The Genealogy of Morals*: 'All terms which semiotically condense a whole process elude definition; only that which has no history can be defined.' We must give up about man (as much as about other animals) the thought that 'species' is a definable term from which we can draw forth our proper purposes. Nietzsche uses the metaphor 'bridge' to describe the human process. Men are a bridge between the beasts from which we came and what we may yet be, if we should overcome being simply men.

The historical sense is more precise than a general recognition of the change in and between the civilizations which make up that bridge. It is the apprehension that in the shortest moment we are never the same, nor are we ever in the presence of the same. Put negatively, in the historical sense we admit the absence of any permanence in terms of which change can be measured or limited or defined. In Nietzsche's ironic phrase, we are required to accept the finality of becoming. Belief in permanence in the world around us arises from the different rhythms of change – for example, in roses, in birds, in stones. Belief in permanence in ourselves (for example, that we are 'selves' or even 'souls') arises from our desire to believe that there is some unifying purpose in our existing. The desire to assert some permanence is particularly pressing among those who have begun to be aware of the abysmal void of its absence, and who wish to turn away from such a cause of fright. The reasonable activities of scientists and philosophers are the attempt to impose some order, so that awareness of primal chaos may be mitigated whether through practical or contemplative ordering. The very language centring around the word truth dominated previous Western history because it was the most disciplined attempt to sedate consciousness against the terror and pain of becoming. But when we examine that language scientifically we see that it is made up of a set of metaphors and metonyms which mitigate the chaos by imposing anthropomorphic explanations on everything. The use of the language of 'truth' is an assertion of value about what we consider 'good' and 'evil,' which we will to impose upon ourselves and others.

At the beginning of the nineteenth century the consequences to be drawn from the dawning historical sense had been alleviated for many by the belief in progress. Because they believed that the process of historical change manifested as a whole the growing power of rationality in the race, and because they assumed that rationality was 'good,' they could find in history the purpose of their existing. Scientists had increasingly been able to show that the non-human world could be fully explained without any idea of final purpose; but the idea of purpose was retained as the unfolding of rationality among the species, man. Nietzsche sees that just as natural science has shown that there is no need of the idea of purpose to understand the geneses and developments of the non-human species, so also there are no reasons to justify belief in the goodness of rationality as our given purpose. The belief that increasing rationality is good is just a survival left over from the centuries of Christianity, when men had seen human life grounded in the sovereignty of the divine wisdom, and so considered reason as more than an instrument. Those who had criticized this traditional perspective to death, in the name of modern science and philosophy, still wanted to keep from it the belief in good and evil. They maintained the idea of purpose through the belief in progressive rationality, while freeing themselves from the legacy of philosophy and theology. But can the exaltation of reasoning be maintained when the very meaning of the word 'reason' has been changed in modern science? According to Nietzsche, in the light of the historical sense men have to give up belief not only in the transcendent ground of permanence (God is dead), but also in the moral valuations which accompanied the former, particularly the idea that our existing has its crowning purpose in rationality.

Nietzsche turns with irony to the fact that the centuries of Western belief in rationality as the highest for man finally produced from itself that science which was to show that there is no reason for this belief. The first exaltation of rationality occurred in Platonism (which according to Nietzsche took popular form in Christianity). It identified reason with virtue, and virtue with happiness, and grounded this identification in the primacy of the idea of the Good. Human existing was at its heart to be trusted as good. It therefore exalted truth-seeking as virtue, and the discipline necessary to that ascetic pursuit. From the long history of disciplined truth-seeking in Christianity, there came forth at last the great modern scientists who, in their pursuit of truth, showed that the human and non-human things can be fully understood without the idea of final purpose, or that human nature is properly directed towards rationality. The very greatness of Christianity was to produce its own grave-diggers.

While Nietzsche recognizes that the historical sense is the basis for all valuable science and philosophy, he affirms with equal force that it cast a blight upon living. Great living comes forth from those who are resolute in the face of chaos. Such resolution has been sustained by the horizons within which men lived. Horizons are the absolute presuppositions within which individuals and indeed whole civilizations do their living. He uses the metaphor 'horizons' because everything which appears, appears to us within their limits. The lives of ordinary men are lived from within their horizons; the deeds of historical men, such as Caesar or Napoleon, come forth from the strength of their horizons. The greatest have been those such as Socrates, the Buddha, or Christ, who have themselves created horizons, within which the people of whole civilizations have henceforth lived.

The historical sense shows us that all horizons are simply the creations of men. In the past, men thought that their horizons were true statements about reality. For example, they affirmed that ultimate reality was reason or love. In terms of these statements, which they considered 'true,' they thought they could know what human purposes were worth pursuing. For example, God being self-giving weakness, the highest human virtue is to give oneself away. But what the historical sense makes plain is that these horizons are not what they claimed to be; they are not true statements about actuality. They are man-made perspectives by which the charismatic impose their will to power. The historical sense teaches us that horizons are not discoveries about the nature of things; they express the values which our tortured instincts will to create.

Nietzsche affirms that once we know that horizons are relative and man-made, their power to sustain us is blighted. Once we know them to be relative, they no longer horizon us. We cannot live in an horizon when we know it to be one. When the historical sense teaches us that our values are not sustained in the nature of things, impotence descends. Nietzsche's most famous aphorism, 'God is Dead,' implies that God was once alive. He was alive in the sense that He was the horizon from which men could know what was worth doing and therefore be sustained in the resolute doing of it. When it is recognized that God is an horizon, He is dead, once and for all. Indeed the death of the Christian God in Western civilization is not just the death of one horizon, it is the end of all horizons. The Christian God might be called the last horizon, because its formidable confidence in truth-seeking as the way of contending with the primal anguish brought forth that science and critical philosophy which have made evident that all horizons are man-made. Nietzsche does not take the death of God – the end of all horizons – as a moment to be taken lightly, as something after which we can get on with the business of making life cosy. He is not the American liberal described by Abbie Hoffman as saying: 'God is dead and we did it for the kids.' For Nietzsche, the end of horizons is not cosy, because we are still left with how to live when we have admitted chaos.

When Nietzsche writes 'only that which has no history can be defined' it may seem that this has little importance outside the logic of definition – an academic matter. Science does not need definitions except as instruments. But 'to define' in a wider context includes stating the purpose of something. The definition of man as the rational animal asserted that our special purpose was rationality. To have been told that man is the creature of Trinity was to know that our highest activity was loving. To say that man has a history and therefore cannot be defined is to say that we can know nothing about what we are fitted for. We make ourselves as we go along. This is what Nietzsche means when he says that we are at the end of the era of rational man. We must live in the knowledge that our purposes are simply creations of human will and not ingrained in the nature of things. But what a burden falls upon the will when the horizons of definition are gone. This is the burden that Nietzsche sees the historical sense imposing on man. On the one hand, we cannot deny history and retreat into a destroyed past. On the other hand, how can we overcome the blighting effect of living without horizons? In his twenties Nietzsche saw the crisis with which the conception of time as history presented men. The great writings of his maturity were his attempt to overcome it.

4

Nietzsche:
Revenge and Redemption

In the last section of *Thus Spoke Zarathustra*, Nietzsche wrote: 'The hour in which I tremble and in which I freeze; the hour which demands and demands and goes on always demanding; "Who has enough courage for that, who deserve to be the masters of the earth?"' In the eighty years since Nietzsche stopped writing, the realized fruits of that drive to mastery are pressed upon us in every day of our lives. Capabilities of mastery over human and non-human beings proliferate, along with reactions by both against that mastering. The historical sense comes from the same intellectual matrix as does the drive to mastery. We have been taught to recognize as illusion the old belief that our purposes are ingrained and sustained in the nature of things. Mastery comes at the same time as the recognition that horizons are only horizons. Most men, when they face that their purposes are not cosmically sustained, find that a darkness falls upon their wills. This is the crisis of the modern world to Nietzsche. The capabilities for mastery present men with a more pressing need of wisdom than any previous circumstances. Who will deserve to be those masters? Who will be wise enough? What is wisdom when reason cannot teach us of human excellence? What is wisdom when we have been taught by the historical sense the finality of becoming? What is wisdom, when we have overcome the idea of eternity?

Till recently it was assumed that our mastery of the earth would be used to promote the values of freedom, rationality, and equality – that is, the values of social democracy. Social democracy was the highest political wisdom. It was to be the guaranteed culmination of history as progress. But to repeat: for Nietzsche progress was the doctrine that held men when the conception of history in Western Christianity had been secularized by modern philosophy and science. Christianity was Platonism for the people. Platonism was the first rationalism. Its identification of rationality, virtue, and happiness was a prodigious affirmation of optimism. This identification was for the few who could reach it in the practice of philosophy. Christianity took this optimism and laid it open to the masses, who could attain it through trust in the creating and redeeming Triune God. It united the identification of reason, virtue, and happiness with the idea of equality, sustained in the fact that all men were created by God and sought by Him in redemption. By this addition of equality, the rationalism was made even more optimistic. In the modern era, that doctrine was secularized: that is, it came to be believed that this uniting of reason and virtue and happiness was not grounded beyond the world in the Kingdom of God, but was coming to be here on earth, in history. By saying that this union was to be realized here on earth, the height of optimism was reached.

In the last part of *Zarathustra* Nietzsche writes: 'The masses blink and say: "We are all equal. – Man is but man, before God – we are all equal." Before God! But now this God has died.' The modern movements that believe in progress towards social democracy assert the equality of all men and a politics based on it. But the same liberal movements have also at their heart that secularism that excludes belief in God. What kind of reason or evidence then sustains the belief that men are equal?

As for the expectations from the progress of knowledge –
that is the belief that freedom will be given its content by men
being open to the truths of science and philosophy – Nietzsche
asserts that we have come to the end of the age of rational
man. To repeat: the cause of this end is the ambiguity at the heart
of science. For Nietzsche, modern science is the height of
modern truthfulness and the centre of our destiny. But it is an
ambiguous centre, because in the very name of 'truthfulness'
– itself a moral value – it has made plain that the values of
rationalism are not cosmically sustained. The natural science
of Darwin and Newton has shown us that nature can be understood without the idea of final purpose. In that understanding,
nature appears to us as indifferent to moral good and evil. We
can control nature; but it does not sustain virtue. As for the
sciences of man, they have shown us that reason is only an
instrument and cannot teach us how it is best to live. In openness to science we learn that nature is morally indifferent, and
that reason is simply an instrument.

At the end of the era of 'rational' man, the public world will
be dominated by two types, whom Nietzsche calls the last
men and the nihilists. The last men are those who have inherited the ideas of happiness and equality from the doctrine of
progress. But because this happiness is to be realized by all
men, the conception of its content has to be shrunk to fit what
can be realized by all. The sights for human fulfilment have to
be lowered. Happiness can be achieved, but only at the cost of
emasculating men of all potentialities for nobility and greatness. The last men will gradually come to be the majority in
any realized technical society. Nietzsche's description of these
last men in *Zarathustra* has perhaps more meaning in us and
for us than it had for his contemporaries who read it in 1883.
'They have their little pleasure for the day and their little pleasure for the night: but they respect health. "We have discovered happiness," say the last men and blink.' [The fun society]
Or again, 'A little poison now and then: that produces pleasant

dreams. And a lot of poison at last, for a pleasant death.' [With Timothy Leary as the priest] Or again, 'Formerly all the world was mad, say the most acute of the last men and blink. They are clever and know everything that has ever happened: so there is no end to their mockery. They still quarrel, but they soon make up – otherwise they might have indigestion' – our intellectuals. The central fact about the last men is that they cannot despise themselves. Because they cannot despise themselves, they cannot rise above a petty view of happiness. They can thus inoculate themselves against the abyss of existing. They are the *last* men because they have inherited rationalism only in its last and decadent form. They think they have emancipated themselves from Christianity; in fact they are the products of Christianity in its secularized form. They will be the growing majority in the northern hemisphere as the modern age unfolds. The little they ask of life (only entertainment and comfort) will give them endurance. This is the price the race has to pay for overcoming two millennia of Christianity.

The end of rational man brings forth not only last men but nihilists. These are those who understand that they can know nothing about what is good to will. Because of the historical sense, they know that all values are relative and man-made; the highest values of the past have devaluated themselves. Men have no given content for their willing. But because men are wills, the strong cannot give up willing.[1] Men would rather will nothing than have nothing to will. Nietzsche clearly has more sympathy for the nihilists than for the last men, because the former put truthfulness above the debased vision of happiness, and in this hold on to the negative side of human greatness. But he has little doubt of the violence and cataclysms that will come forth from men who would rather will nothing than have nothing to will. They will be resolute in their will to mastery,

---

1 Who ever more agreed with St Augustine's dictum *'Quid sumus nisi voluntates?'* [What are we except wills?]

but they cannot know what that mastery is for. The violence of their mastery over human and non-human beings will be without end. In the 1880s he looked ahead to that age of world wars and continued upheavals that most of us in this century have tried to endure.

In parenthesis: if we look at the crises of the modern world through Nietzsche's eyes, and see them above all as the end of two millennia of rational man, we can see that those crises have come to North America later than to Europe. But now that they have come, they are here with intensity. The optimism of rational man was sustained for us in the expectations of the pioneering moment. It was also sustained by the fact that among most of our population our identification of virtue and happiness took the earlier and more virile form that came out of Biblical religion, rather than the soft definition of that identification in the liberalisms of the last men. Among the early majority this was above all Protestant; but its virility was sustained in the Catholicism and Judaism of the later immigrants. In the fresh innocence of North America these religions maintained their force, albeit in primitive form, longer than they did in the more sophisticated Europe. Because the identification of virtue and reason and happiness in these religions was not altogether immanent in its expectations, it held back many North Americans for longer from that banal view of happiness that is the mark of liberalism. As these religions provided some protection from the historical sense, they still provided horizons for our willing that saved the resolute from nihilism. At the height of our present imperial destiny, the crisis of the end of modern rationalism falls upon us ineluctably. In Nietzsche's words: 'the wasteland grows.' The last men and the nihilists are everywhere in North America.

For Nietzsche, there is no possibility of returning to the greatness and glory of pre-rational times, to the age of myth and cult. The highest vision of what men have yet been was unfolded in the early Greek tragedies. Here was laid forth pub-

licly and in ordered form the ecstasy of the suffering and knowing encounter of the noblest men and women with the chaos
of existing. The rationalism of Socrates smoothed away that
encounter by proclaiming the primacy of the idea of the Good,
and in so doing deprived men of the possibility of their greatest height. The optimism of philosophy destroyed the ecstatic
nobility that had been expressed in the tragedies. But now that
rationalism has dug its own grave through the truthfulness of
science, there is no returning to that earlier height. The heritage of rationalism remains in its very overcoming. Its practical heritage is that through technique and experimental science
men are becoming the masters of the earth. Its theoretical heritage is that men now know that nature is indifferent to their
purposes and that they create their own values. Therefore the
question for our species is: can we reach a new height that takes
into itself not only the ecstasy of a noble encounter with chaos,
but also the results of the long history of rationalism? Neither
the nihilists nor the last men deserve to be masters of the earth.
The nihilists only go on willing for the sake of willing. They
assuage their restlessness by involvement in mastery for its
own sake. They are unable to use their mastery for joy. The
last men simply use the fruits of technique for the bored pursuit
of their trivial vision of happiness. The question is whether there
can be men who transcend the alternatives of being nihilists or
last men; who know that they are the creators of their own
values, but bring forth from that creation in the face of chaos a
joy in their willing that will make them deserving of being
masters of the earth.

It must be said that for Nietzsche this crisis is authentic,
because there is no necessity about its outcome. This may be
compared with another influential account of the modern crisis, that of Marx. For Marx also, industrial society is at a turning point. The achievements of capitalism have led to the stage
where this form of social organization must now be transcended. For Marx, as for Nietzsche, this is a situation that produces

widespread and terrible human suffering. But according to
Marx, if we have knowledge of the forces now at work, we
can know that the crisis will inevitably be transcended. In the
midst of the suffering we have that enormous consolation and
spur to effort. A net of inevitable success is put under the per-
formers, so that their actions are guaranteed from the ultimate
anguish. For Nietzsche there is no such net. The historical
sense shows us that we must take seriously the idea that we
create history, and that therefore there can be no inevitable
outcome. We do not know whether beings will appear who
will so overcome themselves that they will deserve to be masters of the earth; we do not know whether the last men will be
in charge for centuries and centuries. To repeat: for Nietzsche
the net of inevitable progress is a shallow secular form of the
belief in God. Just as the historical sense has killed God, it
kills the secular descendants of that belief. Indeed the first
step in man's self-overcoming is to know that all such nets
over chaos are simply comforting illusions. The historical sense
teaches us that what happens now and what will happen is
radically contingent. (I may be allowed to note that the absence
of all nets is a truth that those of us who trust in God must
affirm.)

Unfortunately, one of the key words in Nietzsche's answer
has been killed amongst us by strangely diverse associations.
Most of us on this continent grew up with the comic strips and
film cartoons in which the bespectacled newspaper man, Clark
Kent, turned into 'Superman,' who went zooming through the
skies destroying gangsters and enemies of his country. To use
the word 'superman' is to think that image – an image from
the comics and the Saturday matinee filled with screaming
children and popcorn.

The other association is a debased one. The word 'superman'
was used by the propagandists of the most disgusting political
regime that the Western world has yet produced. The Nazis took
over this part of Nietzsche's language, so that when people of

my generation hear the word 'superman' as used about reality, we conjure up images of those arrogant and sadistic maniacs sweeping their violence and vulgarity over Europe. Because of those events, the word 'superman' has become revolting. Of course, without doubt, Nietzsche would have seen in the Nazis his worst predictions of nihilism and vulgarity combined – predictions that he made particularly about his own people – the Germans.

Indeed as I have watched Leni Riefenstahl's famous documentaries of the Nazi era, particularly her shots of Hitler speaking, I have been aware in Hitler of just that spirit that Nietzsche believes to be the very curse of mankind – the spirit of revenge, (that which in Nietzsche's language above all holds back men from becoming 'supermen' – *Übermenschen*). As one watches Hitler speaking one sees that his effectiveness came from the uniting of his own hysterical self-pity with the same feelings present in his German audience. Life has been a field of pain and defeat for him both privately and publicly, as it has been for the Germans, and he summons up their *ressentiment*.[2] In a political context, Hitler made specific demands; but behind anything specific one feels a demand more universal – a demand for unlimited revenge. This is what Nietzsche says is the very basis for the violence of nihilism. Indeed in his language, the supermen will be those who have overcome in themselves any desire for revenge. As he writes in *Zarathustra*: 'That man may be delivered from revenge: that is for me the bridge to the highest hope.'

(To make a parenthesis about Leni Riefenstahl's films: many people these days seem to place enormous confidence in the electronic media. They see in them the way by which enlightenment can be brought to the majority. Electronic enlightenment will overcome the old anal rationality of print and speech.

---

2 'Resentment,' but Nietzsche used the French term because he thought there was no equivalent in German. *Ed.*

Those who think this way should ponder these films of Leni Riefenstahl. The art of the film was there used in all its stunning magic. But these films were made to persuade men of the glory of the most base of political regimes. Indeed to watch them is to be presented with Nietzsche's very question: Who deserves to be the master of electronics? [Is it] The last men and nihilists from contemporary television journalism and politics? One would be happier about the McLuhanite cult, if its members dealt with such questions.)

Both because of the comic strip and because of the Nazis, the word superman cannot be used with seriousness amongst us. But that fact must not prevent us from looking at Nietzsche's question. Who is wise enough for this moment in history? Nietzsche takes the historical sense for granted. He does not speak of the race of men as if they had a nature that is unchanging through the course of history. Man is a bridge between the beasts and something higher than man. As he writes in *Beyond Good and Evil*: 'Man is the as yet undetermined animal.' It is now open to man in the future to become nobler than his past, so that some will come to deserve the present destiny of being masters of the planet. For this deserving, the essential condition is that men overcome the spirit of revenge. Therefore if one wants to understand what Nietzsche means by history, one must look at what he means by revenge.

Desire for revenge has come from the very conditions of human existence. As self-conscious animals men have lived in the chaotic world, experiencing as anguish all its accidents, its terrors, and its purposelessness. Most men have lived in a world in which our instincts are thwarted and twisted from the very moment we enter it. Our wills are continually broken on the wheel of the chaos that is the world. Our response to that brokenness is the will to revenge against others, against ourselves, against the very condition of time itself. 'It is the body that has despaired of the body.' From that despair comes forth the spirit of revenge. The more botched and bungled our instincts become in the vicissitudes of existing, the greater our will to revenge on what has been done us.

Nietzsche was the first to use consistently that description of man that Freud later employed for psychoanalysis. The elemental in man is an 'it,' that is, an impersonal chaos of instincts out of which comes forth as epiphenomena, reason and morality. It was once believed that the irrational in man existed to be subordinated to the rational. In Nietzsche this is denied. This does not, however, free us from thinking. It simply means that thinking is carried on over an abyss that it can never fathom. Philosophy is simply the highest from of 'the will to power.' As he writes in *Beyond Good and Evil*: There is a point in every philosophy when the philosopher's conviction appears on the stage – or to use the language of an ancient Mystery:

> Adventavit asinus,
> Pulcher et fortissimus.[3]

Nietzsche enucleates with black wit the many forms of revenge that make up for him the very substance of history. In the earliest societies, the victory of the strong over the weak is the victory of those with vigorous instincts over the majority of weak instinct. The weak bring forth from their condition of enslavement the spirit of revenge. The rules of justice come from that spirit. The creditor takes a quantum of revenge for the debtor who cannot meet his debts. As the infliction of pain gives pleasure, the creditor finds his satisfaction in that punishment. In the West, the greatest achievement of the spirit of revenge has been Christianity. In it, the priests, who are those among the ruling classes whose instincts have been most botched and bungled, and therefore desire the greatest revenge, get power by uniting with the weak majority against

---

3 'The ass (or blockhead) came along, fair (or admirable) and supremely audacious.' *Ed.*

the strong. They produce a morality that exalts such virtues as altruism, humility, equality, etc. Those virtues necessary anyway for the weak majority are guaranteed to get them revenge, in the next world, if not in this. The priests teach an ascetic morality, telling men that the instincts should be repressed. In the name of this rationalist control, those of strong and noble instinct are held back from their proper authority for the sake of the weak and bungled majority.

Indeed, the will to revenge is turned inward by men against themselves. They punish themselves, not only others. The greed of the self teaches us that if we put aside full living in the name of humility and altruism and asceticism, we will gain an infinite extension of our wills in eternity. Those who transpose their will from this world to the beyond are expressing the most intense will to power out of their desire for revenge at not being able to express it in this life. For Nietzsche the very idea of transcendence – that time is enfolded in eternity – is produced out of the spirit of revenge by those who because of their broken instincts are impotent to live in the world, and in their self-pity extrapolate to a non-existent perfection in which their failures will be made good. In the language I have used in these lectures, any belief that time cannot be identified with history comes from the broken instincts of men who cannot live greatly in history. For Nietzsche, Plato is the philosophic enemy, because he conceives time as an image, 'the moving image of eternity.' The reality of the 'idea' was invented by Socrates, who wanted to overcome tragedy and who therefore posited that the immediate world was just the moving image of a real eternity. The greatness of Socrates was the greatness of his revenge on tragedy. But philosophy only provided revenge for the few. In Christianity the will to revenge is taken up into a transcendence opened to the majority. As Nietzsche puts it in *The Genealogy of Morals*: 'Then suddenly we come face to face with that paradoxical and ghastly expedient, which brought temporary relief to tortured humanity, that most brilliant stroke of Christianity: God's sacrifice of himself for man. God makes himself the ransom for what could not otherwise be ransomed; God alone has power to absolve us of a debt we can no longer discharge; the creditor offers himself as a sacrifice for his debtor out of sheer love (can you believe it) out of love for his debtor.'

Now that Christianity has been secularized, the transcendence of progress has been substituted for the transcendence of God. The spirit of revenge is still at work among the last men and the nihilists. The last men want revenge against anything that is noble and great, against anything that threatens their expectations from triviality. The nihilists want revenge on the fact that they cannot live with joy in the world. Their revenge takes the form of restless violence against any present. As nothingness is always before them, they seek to fill the void by willing for willing's sake. There can be no end to their drive for mastery.

Indeed for Nietzsche, revenge arises most deeply in our recognition that all our existing is subject to time's thrall. Everything is enfolded in 'it was,' 'it is,' 'it will be.' And as we recognize that inescapable temporality in every lived minute, we can will to batter against its inevitable consequences. That is the deepest cause of our revengings. At its simplest, we want revenge against what is present in our present. If we seek to overcome our present by bending our efforts to the building of a future to suit our heart's desire, when that future came we would still be subject to that thrall. At the deepest level, revenge is most engaged against the past. [That is what Professor Marcuse cannot include within his utopian marxism.] Consciousness always includes within itself 'it was.' Human life would not be possible without some memory. But the will can do nothing about the past. What has happened has happened, and we cannot change it. By the 'it was' of time, Nietzsche means not only our personal past (with its defeats, its enslavements, its tortured instincts), but the past of the race that is opened to us in communal memory, and opened to us as never before by the historical sense. [As a great thinker of this century[4] has said to her fellow Christians: 'Can we make object(s) of contemplation out of 70,000 slaves hanging on their crosses on the roads about Rome after the defeat of the slave rebellion?' How does the will overcome its desire for revenge on that past?] In *Zarathustra* Nietzsche writes: 'To transform every "it was" into "this is what I wanted" – that alone I could call redemption.' The height is for him *amor fati*.[5] And that love must come out of having grasped into one's consciousness the worst that can be remembered or imagined – the torturing of children and the screams of the innocent.

To deserve to be masters of the earth will be to have overcome the spirit of revenge and therefore to be able to will and create in joy. Nietzsche's image for himself is the convalescent. He is recovering, step by step, from the spirit of revenge. The recovery from that sickness is not simply from the disasters of his own instincts, but the recovery from the long history of revenge in the race. In that history, the greatest revenge against time's 'it was' took the form of belief in the transcendence of a timeless eternity. It pretended to be a redemption of time, but it was in fact an expression of revenge against time. To live on the earth, to be masters of the earth, to deserve to be masters because we can live in joy, requires the act of *amor fati*, held outside any assertion of timelessness. The love of fate has been asserted in the Greek tragedies, in Plato, and by certain Christians. But this fate was enfolded in a timeless eternity, in an ultimate perfection. For Nietzsche, the achievement of *amor fati* must be outside any such enfoldment. It must be willed in a world where there is no possibility of either an infinite or finite transcendence of becoming or of willing.

4 Simone Weil. *Ed.*
5 Love of fate. *Ed.*

For Nietzsche, the possibility of that love of fate is related to his discovery of 'the eternal recurrence of the identical.' This 'discovery' was that as the number of possible combinations of what exists is finite, yet time is infinite; there has already been and will be again an endless recurrence of the present state of affairs, and of every other state possible. As he writes in *Zarathustra*:

> You do not know my abysmal thought – that thought which you could not endure.
>
> Look at this gateway. – Two paths come together here and no one has ever reached their end.
>
> This long path behind us goes on for an eternity. And that long path ahead of us – that is another eternity. –
>
> On the gateway is written its name: Moment.
>
> –
>
> Must not all things that can run have already run along this path? Must not all things that can happen have already happened, been done, run past?
>
> And if all things have been here before; what do you think of this moment? – Must not this gateway, too, have been here, before?
>
> And are not all things bound inextricably together in such a way that this moment draws after it all future things? Therefore, draws itself too?
>
> For all things that can run must also run once again forward along this long path.
>
> And this slow spider that creeps along in the moonlight, and this moonlight itself and both of us at this gateway whispering together – must we not all have been here before
>
> – and must we not return and run down that other path before us, down that long terrible path – must we not return eternally?
>
> This is what I said and I said it more and more softly: for I was afraid of my own thoughts and reservations.

It is not my business to repeat here all that Nietzsche says about that 'discovery.' It can be found in *Zarathustra* and in his notebooks, which have been published posthumously in English under the title *The Will to Power*. Nor is it my task to write here of the objections which have been made against 'the eternal recurrence of the identical' – that is, to discuss the varied thoughts of those who claim that it is not a discovery. However, I can say that in the endurance of that 'discovery' Nietzsche found the possibility of overcoming the spirit of revenge. In that thoughtful enduring was the movement towards the realization of *amor fati*. According to Nietzsche, when men know themselves beyond good and evil, the strong are moved to the violence of an undirected willing of novelty. But from his 'discovery' Nietzsche's nihilism becomes therapeutic, so that he can begin to will novelty in joy. In the recognition of the dominance of time in which no past is past and no future has not yet been and yet in which there is openness to the immediate future – the conception of time as history reaches its height and yet is not hypostatized into a comforting horizon.

5

Time as Mastery

I have brushed against the writings of Nietzsche because he has thought the conception of time as history more comprehensively than any other thinker. He lays bare the fate of technical man, not as an object held in front of us, but as that in which our very selves are involved in the proofs of the science that lays it bare. In thinking the modern project, he did not turn away from it. His critical wit about modern society might lead one to believe that he condemned its assumptions. Rather he expressed the contradictions and difficulties in the thought and life of Western civilization, not for the sake of turning men away from that enterprise, but so that they could overcome its difficulties and fulfil its potential heights. In his work, the themes that must be thought in thinking time as history are raised to a beautiful explicitness: the mastery of human and non-human nature in experimental science and technique, the primacy of the will, man as the creator of his own values, the finality of becoming, the assertion that potentiality is higher than actuality, that motion is nobler than rest, that dynamism rather than peace is the height. The simpler things that Nietzsche says (for example, that men must now live without the comfort of horizons) seem so obvious to most people today that

they are hardly worth emphasizing. Everybody uses the word
'values' to describe our making of the world: capitalists and
socialists, atheists and avowed believers, scientists and politi-
cians. The word comes to us so platitudinously that we take it
to belong to the way things are. It is forgotten that before
Nietzsche and his immediate predecessors, men did not think
about their actions in that language. They did not think they
made the world valuable, but that they participated in its goodness. What is comic about the present use of 'values,' and the
distinction of them from 'facts,' is not that it is employed by
modern men who know what is entailed in so doing, but that it
is used also by 'religious' believers who are unaware that in
its employment they are contradicting the very possibility of
the reverence they believe they are espousing in its use. The
reading of Nietzsche would make that clear to them. Indeed
even some of the deeper aspects of Nietzsche's thought
increasingly become explicit in our world. If one listens carefully to the revolt of the noblest young against bourgeois America, one hears deeper notes in it than were ever sounded by
Marx, and those are above all the notes of Nietzsche.

To repeat: the thought of great thinkers is not a matter for
the chit-chat of television and cocktail parties; nor for provid-
ing jobs for academics in the culture industry. In it the fate of
our whole living is expressed. In this sense, the thought of
Nietzsche is a fate for modern men. In partaking in it, we can
come to make judgments about the modern project – that enormous enterprise that came out of western Europe in the last
centuries and has now become worldwide.

Nevertheless, as implied in the previous pages, the conception of time as history is not one in which I think life can be
lived properly. It is not a conception we are fitted for. Therefore I turn away from Nietzsche and in so turning express my
suspicion of the assumptions of the modern project. Yet this
immediately produces a difficulty. Before speaking against
Nietzsche, one must affirm the language one shares with him,

even as one negates his use of it. To illustrate: Nietzsche clearly uses the same language as the tradition in its eternal truth, when he says that the height for human beings is *amor fati*. Yet the love of fate, which he would call redemption, is not in any sense a call to the passivity that some moderns falsely identify with words such as 'fate' or 'destiny.' In him the love of fate is at one with his call to dynamic willing. The love of fate is the guarantee that dynamic willing shall be carried on by lovers of the earth, and not by those twisted by hatred and hysteria against existing (however buried that hysteria may be in the recesses of our instincts). Some marxists have taken his love of fate as if it were a call to passivity as the height, and as if, therefore, he were an essentially non-political writer. They have denied that love of fate (love of the injustices and alienations and exploitations of time) can be good. Is it not just a sufficiently deep and sustained hatred of these iniquities that brings men to fight and to overcome them? But Nietzsche's love of fate is not passive, but a call to dynamic political doing. He states explicitly that any philosophy must finally be judged in the light of its political recommendations. What he is saying beyond many marxists is that the building of the potential height in modern society can only be achieved by those who have overcome revenge, so that what they accomplish comes forth from a positive love of the earth, and not simply from hatred of what presently is. Dynamic willing that has not overcome revenge will always have the marks of hysteria and hatred within it. It can only produce the technical frenzy of the nihilists or the shallow goals of the last men. It cannot come to terms with the questions: 'what for, whither and what then?' However, against the complacency of any easy *amor fati*, Nietzsche makes clear that it must take into itself all the pain and anguish and ghastliness that has ever been, and also the loathing of that ghastliness and pain. Hatred against existence is, it would seem, limitless, and the more we are aware of the nervous systems of others, the more that hatred and hysteria must be actual or repressed for us. Only those of us who are not much open to others can readily claim that we think existing to be as we wanted it. *Amor fati* is then a height for men, not in the sense that it is easily achieved or perhaps ever achieved by any human being. The redemption that Nietzsche holds forth is not cheaply bought.

Yet having said this, I must state my simple incomprehension. How is it possible to assert the love of fate as the height and, at the same time, the finality of becoming? I do not understand how anybody could love fate, unless within the details of our fates there could appear, however rarely, intimations that they are illumined; intimations, that is, of perfection (call it if you will God) in which our desires for good find their rest and their fulfilment. I do not say anything about the relation of that perfection to the necessities of existing, except that there must be some relation; nor do I state how or when the light of that perfection could break into the ambiguities and afflictions of any particular person. I simply state the argument for perfection (sometimes called the ontological argument): namely, that human beings are not beyond good and evil, and that the desire for good is a broken hope without perfection, because only the desire to become perfect does in fact make us less imperfect. This means that the absurdities of time – its joys as well as its diremptions – are to be taken not simply as history, but as enfolded in an unchanging meaning, which is untouched by potentiality or change. So when Nietzsche affirms that *amor fati* comes forth from the contemplation of the eternity (not timelessness, but endless time) of the creating and destroying powers of man and the rest of nature, I do not understand how that could be a light that would free us from the spirit of revenge. It seems to me a vision that would drive men mad – not in the sense of a divine madness, but a madness destructive of good.

[That we must speak of two accounts of reason, the ancient and the modern, can be seen in the fact that for the ancients thought was at its height, not in action, but in what they called a passion. Whatever the differences in what came to us from Jerusalem and from Athens, on this central point there was a commonness. The height for man was a passion. In modern language we may weakly describe this by saying that thought was finally a receptivity. We can see that this is not true of modern thought because its very form is the making of hypotheses and the testing by experiment, something intimately connected with the acts of our wills, the controlling of the world, the making of history.

Indeed, the enormous difficulty of thinking outside the modern account of thought is seen in my using the very word 'passion.' Words that once summoned up receptivity have disappeared or disintegrated into triviality. If I were to use the noblest Greek word for this receptivity, *pathos,* and say, as has been said, that philosophy arises from the *pathos* of astonishment, the suffering of astonishment, the word would bear no relation to our present use of it.]

The preceding statements are not here proved or even argued. Indeed it is questionable how much it would be possible to argue them in the modern world. For all those statements are made from out of an ancient way of thinking. And to repeat: the core of the intellectual history of the last centuries has been the criticism of that ancient account of thought. As that criticism has publicly succeeded, what comes to us from that ancient thought is generally received as unintelligible and simply arbitrary. All of us are increasingly enclosed by the modern account. For example, central to my affirmations in the previous paragraph are the propositions: the core of our lives is the desire for perfection, and only that desire can make us less imperfect. Yet clearly that account of 'morality' (to use a modern word) is quite different from what has been affirmed about morality in the last centuries. The attempt to argue for my propositions would require a very close historical analysis of how the use of such words as 'desire' and 'reason' have changed over the last centuries. It would require, for example, what the ancients meant by 'passion.' Whatever the differences between what has come to us from Plato and from Christianity, on this central point there is commonness. The height for man could only come forth out of a passion. Yet in using such a word, the enormous difficulty of thinking outside the modern account can be seen. When we use the word 'pathetic' we may be thinking of a defeated character in a movie [like Ratso in *Midnight Cowboy*], or the performance of the quarterback for the Hamilton Tiger Cats football team this season. [As for the word suffering, that means simply pain, which sensible men have always wished to avoid.] The word 'passion' has come to be limited for us to little more than an emotion of driving force, particularly intense sexual excitement. [The experiences of receptivity having dropped from our vocabulary, we think of art and thought and morality quite differently. We talk of what the artist does as creation, not as imitation, a begetting of the beautiful.] To say that philosophy arises from the suffering of astonishment would bear no relation to our present understanding of thought, because the archetype of thought is now that science that frames instrumental hypotheses and tests them in experiment, a kind of willing. How can we think of morality as a desiring attention to perfection, when for the last centuries the greatest moral philosophers have written of it as self-legislation, the willing of our own values? Therefore my affirmations in the previous paragraph use language in a way that can hardly be appropriated. [As an example of the poverty of modern language, let me say how partial it is to speak of Tolstoy as creating *War and Peace*, or Mozart his piano concertos. The disappearance of the words of receptivity, the words of passion, from the modern account of thought, shows what a wide separation there is between the ancient and the modern. It clarifies what it means to say that modern thinking is always a kind of willing. Because we are always surrounded in every conscious minute of our lives by the modern conception of thought, we cannot take what is given to us from the past as intelligible. If we take it at all, we take it more and more as sheerly arbitrary. Therefore fewer and fewer people can appropriate it.]

Indeed, beyond this, there is a further turn of the screw for anybody who would assert that *amor fati* is the height, yet cannot understand how that height could be achievable outside the vision of our fate as enfolded in a timeless eternity. The destruction of the idea of such an eternity has been at the centre of the modern project in the very scientific and technical mastery of chance. As a great contemporary, Leo Strauss, has written in *What Is Political Philosophy?*: 'Oblivion of eternity, or, in other words, estrangement from man's deepest desire and therewith from the primary issues, is the price that modern man had to pay, from the very beginning, for attempting to be absolutely sovereign, to become the master and owner of nature, to conquer chance.' And the turn of the screw is that to love fate must obviously include loving the fate that makes us part of the modern project; it must include loving that which has made us oblivious of eternity – that eternity without which I cannot understand how it would be possible to love fate.

To put the matter simply: any appeal to the past must not be made outside a full recognition of the present. Any use of the past that insulates us from living now is cowardly, trivializing, and at worst despairing. Antiquarianism can be used like most other drugs as mind contracting. If we live in the present we must know that we live in a civilization, the fate of which is to conceive time as history. Therefore as living now, the task of thought among those held by something that cannot allow them to make the complete 'yes' to time as history, is not to inoculate themselves against their present, but first to enter what is thought in that present.

What has happened in the West since 1945 concerning the thought of Marx is an example of inoculation. Our chief rival empire has been ruled by men who used Marx's doctrine as their official language, while we used an earlier form of modernity, the liberalism of capitalist democracy. The thought of Marx, therefore, appeared as a threatening and subverting disease. The intellectual industry in our multiversities produced a spate of refutations of Marx. Most of these, however, were written with the purpose of inoculating others against any contagion, rather than with thinking the thoughts that Marx had thought. These books have not prevented the reviving influence of Marx's thought among many of the brightest young, any more than the official marxism of the East has been able to stop the influence of existentialism among its young élites. [Why? Marx's thought abides because he thought some of what is happening in the modern world. His writings could therefore help other men to think about what was happening. What we were doing in Vietnam seemed to be explained by marxism.] Men may have to attempt this inoculation if they are concerned with the stability of a particular society, but it is well to know when one is doing it that it is not concerned directly with philosophy but with public stability. And you will not even be successful at inoculating those most important to inoculate, if you pretend you understand Marx when you do not. To apply the comparison: when I state that I do not understand how Nietzsche could assert *amor fati* to be the height, while at the same time asserting the finality of becoming, my purpose is not to inoculate against Nietzsche. [As I have said, Nietzsche thinks what it is to be a modern man more comprehensively, more deeply, than any other thinker, including Marx, including Freud, including the existentialists, including the positivists. Therefore the first task of somebody trying to think time as history is not to inoculate, but to think his thoughts.] The task of inoculation is best left to those who write textbooks. [Yet if I am right that in the thought of Nietzsche we drink most deeply of the modern experiment, we cannot finally avoid making some judgments of that experiment, and so of that thought. We might start from our current experience, and argue that since Nietzsche's day more evidence is in. As one looks at the vulgar and chaotic results of our modern dynamism, it is possible to say that the modern project has led men away from excellence, and that this debasement is not accidental, but comes forth from the very assumptions of that project. Then one would say that these debasements are not to be overcome by a further extension of the modern assumptions, as Nietzsche would have it. If one denies the possibility of any returning to the past, and yet does not believe in the assumptions of the modern experiment, what then is the task of thought?]

What then could be the position of those who cannot live through time as if it were simply history, who cannot believe that love of fate could be achieved together with the assertion of the finality of becoming, and yet must live in the dynamism of our present society? In that position there is a call to remembering and to loving and to thinking.

What I mean by remembering was expressed for me by a friend who died recently. He knew that he was dying, not in the sense that we all know that this is going to happen sometime. He knew it because a short term had been put upon his life at an early age, long before what he was fitted for could be accomplished. Knowing that he lived in the close presence of his own death, he once said shortly: 'I do not accept Nietzsche.' Clearly such a remark was not intended to express a realized refutation of Nietzsche. Neither he nor I saw ourselves capable of that magisterial task. He had collected (at a time when such collecting must have been pressed upon him) what had been given him about the unfathomable goodness of the whole, from his good fortune in having partaken in a tradition of reverence. In the inadequate modern equivalent for reverence and tradition, his remark might be called 'religious.'

In an age when the primacy of the will, even in thinking, destroys the varied forms of reverence, they must come to us, when and if they come, from out of tradition. 'Tradition' means literally a handing over; or, as it once meant, a surrender. The man who was dying was in his remark surrendering to me his recollection of what had been surrendered to him, from the fortune that had been his, in having lived within a remembered reverence – in his case, Christianity. [He surrendered to me the affirmation that the whole is in some unfathomable sense good. The absurdities of time, indeed also its joys as well as its diremptions, are to be taken not simply as history but as enfolded in a meaning (call it if you will a transcendence) that is beyond potentiality, that is beyond change. I do not imply that what is handed over in tradition must be in conflict with reason or experience. The belief that reason and tradition are at loggerheads is only a product of modern thought. It comes from the doctrine of progress, that the race as a whole is becoming increasingly open to reason by shuffling off its irrational past. The traditions that came to us from Athens and Jerusalem claim to be, in the main, reasonable, but what was handed over in them is now accepted, if accepted at all, less and less as thought-filled because it is so assailed by the modern account of reason, and all of us are increasingly enclosed by that modern account. The core of the history of the last three hundred years has been the criticism of the ancient account of thought and the coming to be of the new account. As that criticism has publicly succeeded, what comes to us from the past is received as unintelligible, as simply arbitrary.] In the presence of death, [my friend] had collected out of that remembrance an assertion for me that stated how he transcended conceiving time as history.

By distinguishing remembering from thinking, I do not imply that this collecting was unthoughtful, but that what this man had there collected could not have been entirely specified in propositions. For nearly everyone (except perhaps for the occasional great thinkers) there is no possibility of entirely escaping that which is given in the public realm, and this increasingly works against the discovery of any reverence. Therefore those of us who at certain times look to grasp something beyond history must search for it as the remembering of a negated tradition and not as a direct thinking of our present. Perhaps reverence belongs to man qua man and is indeed the matrix of human nobility. But those several conceptions, being denied in our present public thought, can themselves only be asserted after they have been sought for through the remembrance of the thought of those who once thought them.

Remembering must obviously be a disciplined activity in a civilization where the institutions that should foster it do not. One form of it may be scholarship, the study of what the past has given us. But scholarship of itself need not be remembering. The scholar may so hold out from himself what is given from the past (that is, so objectify it) that he does not in fact remember it. There are scholars, for example, who have learnt much of the detailed historical and literary background of the Bible, and yet who remember less of what was essentially given in those books than Jews or Christians untutored in such scholarship. This is no argument against the necessity of disciplined scholarship. It is simply the statement that modern scholarship has to hold itself above the great gulf of progressive assumptions, if it is to be more than antiquarian technique and become remembering.

It may also be said that 'remembering' is a misleading word, because we should turn not only to our own origins in Athens and Jerusalem, but to those of the great civilizations of the East. Many young North Americans are learning from Asia, because of the barrenness of their own traditions. Indeed many have only been able to look at their own past because they have first been grasped by something in Asia. It is hardly necessary for a member of a department of religion, such as myself, to assert that it can be a great good for Western people in their time of darkness to contemplate the sources of thought and life as they have been in the East. But that meeting will be only a kind of esoteric game, if it is undertaken to escape the deepest roots of Western fate. We can only come to any real encounter with Asia, if we come in some high recognition of what we inevitably are. I use the word 'remembering' because, wherever else we turn, we cannot turn away from our own fate, which came from our original openings to comedy and tragedy, to thought and charity, to anxiety and shame.

As remembering can only be carried on by means of what is handed over to us, and as what is handed over is a confusion of truth and falsity, remembering is clearly not self-sufficient. Any tradition, even if it be the vehicle by which perfection itself is brought to us, leaves us with the task of appropriating from it, by means of loving and thinking, that which it has carried to us. Individuals, even with the help of their presently faltering institutions, can grasp no more than very small segments of what is there. Nor (to repeat) should any dim apprehensions of what was meant by perfection before the age of progress be used simply as means to negate what may have been given us of truth and goodness in this age. The present darkness is a real darkness, in the sense that the enormous corpus of logistic and science of the last centuries is uncoordinate as to any possible relation it may have to those images of perfection that are given us in the Bible and in philosophy. We must not forget that new potentialities of reasoning and making happen have been actualized (and not simply contemplated as mistrusted potentialities, as for example in Plato) and therefore must be thought as having been actualized, in relation to what is remembered. The conception of time as history is not to be discarded as if it had never been.

It may be that at any time or place, human beings can be opened to the whole in their loving and thinking, even as its complete intelligibility eludes them. If this be true of any time or place, then one is not, after all, trapped in historicism. But now the way to intelligibility is guarded by a more than usual number of ambiguities. Our present is like being lost in the wilderness, when every pine and rock and bay appears to us as both known and unknown, and therefore as uncertain pointers on the way back to human habitation. The sun is hidden by the cloud and the usefulness of our ancient compasses has been put in question. Even what is beautiful – which for most men has been the pulley to lift them out of despair – has been made equivocal for us both in detail and definition. [The very bringing into being of our civilization has put in question the older means of finding one's way, without discovering new means for doing so. Nevertheless it is also clear that this very position of ambiguity in our civilization presents enormous hope for thought, if not for life. The questions whether the modern project opens out new heights for man, or whether at its heart it was a false turning for man, are so clearly before us. Questions that were settled, and therefore closed over the last centuries, are now open to us once again. Perhaps the essential question about the modern project is not that of Nietzsche – Who deserve to be the masters of the earth? – but the very question of mastery itself.]

Nevertheless, those who cannot live as if time were history are called, beyond remembering, to desiring and thinking. But this is to say very little. For myself, as probably for most others, remembering only occasionally can pass over into thinking and loving what is good. It is for the great thinkers and the saints to do more.

Dialogue on the Death of God with Dr Charles Malik

[The Canadian Broadcasting Corporation presented a special sequel to the 1969 Massey Lectures, *Time as History*: a dialogue between George Grant and Dr Charles Malik, Lebanese diplomat, former president of the United Nations General Assembly, and lecturer in Greek Orthodox theology at the American University in Beirut.]

MALIK: Your interest in Nietzsche gives me great pleasure because I have studied Nietzsche in Germany under Heidegger and read the interpretations of Nietzsche by Jaspers and the great thinkers of this age. In addition, of course, I have imbibed Nietzsche at a very early age and was deeply influenced by him. I think you are quite right in saying Nietzsche plays a very important role in the modern firmament of thought. And you put it here that these basic undertones in the modern revolt of youth go back to Nietzsche perhaps more than to any other thinker.

Concerning your interpretation of Nietzsche I may not completely agree with you because I believe Nietzsche was a tremendous rebel against the falsities of Western existence. He could only have been that, as you intimated at one point in your lecture, because of the deep Christian background from which he spoke. I therefore would look upon Nietzsche more as a perverted and inverted Christian prophet (and for that reason a very important man) than a secular philosopher. Let me very briefly, just to touch off some kind of conversation between us two, remark on one or two things in your presentation. First of all, the most important observation I want to make is that you're dealing all the time with forms and concepts and generalities. Now that is part of the malaise of the world against which you seem to be reacting. Therefore I should have wished just from the point of view of refreshment and antithesis, I should have wished you to be far more personal, far less general, far less speaking in terms of tendencies, and concepts, and generalities, and ideas, and far more in terms of individual persons. You named a few people, but you soon dissolved them into their ideas rather than retained their distinctive individuality. This is idealism. And the problem with this world is this excessive idealism. You talk about the youth – the youth are idealists. They are idealists in the bad sense of the term. I wish they were idealists in the good sense of the term. Now you seem, in treating them on their own level, to be confirming them in their false idealism. You had better talk to them in terms of their own persons. And the best way of doing it is to put before them some great personal heroes of history – and I shall come to that in a moment on another level.

Then you say about the past coming to us as unintelligible, as simply arbitrary. I wish you had dwelt more on this because it is this very denial of the reality of the past and the livingness of the past that is part of the great tragedy of Western existence today. It is this disruption of the past, this discontinuity from the past, this breaking away from the past. [Perhaps] here in the new world you feel that is part of your life and you want to forget about Europe and about the old countries and about the old traditions and start out in a new world all of your own. Well, [it could be that] this modern temper has been produced exactly by your own feelings, by your own experiments. You cannot break away from the old world – either intellectually, or spiritually, or certainly these days as you know, politically. The unintelligibility of the past is your own fault, much more than the fault of what you here are criticizing. It is the re-establishment of the unity of the tradition and the making it appear as the only intelligible thing, and as the ground of intelligibility far more than what you call reason. I know you are reacting against it, but I wish you had brought that out much more clearly to show that the ground of reason is a tradition and not only abstract immediate rational considerations.

Then you speak about Christianity, and this is probably the most important thing I want to say. I don't know what you mean by Christianity – I only know what is meant by the church. You don't mention the word church (I don't think you do – you may have mentioned it here and there). But that, you see, in keeping with your generalizing approach, [that] Christianity is a system. Why don't you talk about Jesus of Nazareth? Your young men these days don't want to talk about persons; they want to talk about ideas, systems, Christianity, Hinduism, Western civilization. Well with all respect to Western civilization, Western civilization would have been nothing and probably would be nothing without Jesus Christ. I want to be as specific as that. You can't make a dent on these young men these days if you fall into these generalities. I wish you had spoken about Jesus Christ of Nazareth, who lived and died and said what He said and thought about Himself in the way He thought about Himself and was understood as He was by the church. You know what is going to happen? Western civilization may go to pieces and probably deserves it. But the church isn't going to go to pieces. I can make a prediction now, which you should have made in your lecture – that whatever happens to you in Canada and the United States the Christian church will survive you all. And the Christian church is based upon Jesus of Nazareth, not upon ideas of Christianity. I have no idea what the word Christianity means. The word Christianity varies from one culture to another. But I have every idea what Jesus of Nazareth means.

And finally time as history reminds me, of course, of the second part of Heidegger's *Sein und Zeit*. The tradition, the living tradition, that is the effect that is most needed here – to make people feel that you are dealing with four thousand years of continuous tradition, so that the present [grows] out of the past, and the past out of its own past. Unity of time – unity of history. I wish you had done more.

GPG: I just want to say that North America is the only society that has no history before the age of progress. I remember, when I went to Europe (Europe in my case being England and France), feeling this sense of continuity. I would have enormous sympathy for your sense of particularity, but I would say [that] in the kind of life we have now in North America the tradition is just broken. I think it is incomparably easier for somebody who lives in a great society like the Near East has been, where it is all around you, to understand what it means to live in 4000 years, but in North America Henry Ford had it when he said, 'History is bunk.' And our ancestors were the poor of Western Europe who wanted to get out, and who wanted to turn their back on the tradition and, when they crossed on the ships, they broke that tradition. And I think this is the tragedy of North America. I would certainly believe that the church, as you say, will exist when civilizations have gone. But I think it is a terrible, immediate tragedy that North American progressivism first destroyed Protestantism, then it destroyed Judaism, and now I think indubitably it is destroying Catholicism in North America. I don't mean everywhere. But I think it is destroying it in North America. Now I think it is incredibly difficult for young North Americans. They grow up in a world were everything is new every moment. The tradition is orientation to the future – there is no sense of the past.

The yearning of North Americans for the past and to turn away from the denial of tradition is everywhere. But how you reestablish a tradition in a society like this when it is totally broken I do not know.

MALIK: Well, may I make one or two observations on that very point. You see, the tradition is wholly broken but it is obvious that for the thinking mind, for responsible individuals like yourself and others, for leaders, for statesmen, for thinkers, it's obvious that it cannot be broken. This very language that you are using you did not invent here. You brought it over from abroad and language is the greatest vehicle of culture and tradition. Shakespeare is studied here as much as in England and Shakespeare is the vehicle of the continuity of your tradition. How can you say you started from scratch? You never started from scratch here. Take the Bible. The Bible takes you back four thousand years. The Bible is at the very core and the heart of your civilization here. This is [the] Christmas season – I was seeing your magnificent decorations and illuminations last night here in Toronto. Well, you all are thinking in terms of Bethlehem. I think you will be thinking it for several weeks. That's a very clear thought. With the English language, with the English Bible, with English law, how can you say that you are starting from scratch here? You go back for hundreds of years to your roots in Europe. If you do not acknowledge them, well that is your fault. The objective state of affairs is that you are an offshoot, a continuation, of the European, Western, Mediterranean tradition and you've got to recognize that and reestablish it consciously in your own mind. And your kids who go about as if the world begins with them, they should be told the truth – that the world began before them.

GPG: We came here just at the time when Europe itself, partly in the name of something new, was attacking its tradition. For instance, the science of Galileo and the moral science of

Machiavelli were attacking Aristotle, were attacking the Mediterranean, the Greek side. At the same time there was an enormous attack by these same people against the Biblical side. You can't read people like Locke and Rousseau without seeing that there is a fantastic attack on Christianity going on. Now, what I'm saying is just when the Europeans were secularizing, were kicking out the heart of what I called Athens and Jerusalem, North Americans came across to this continent. And it seems to me the power of what I call modern liberalism – that is, the belief that you are going to build a universal and homogeneous state that eliminates all particularity – has, except for the province of Quebec, built a universal and homogeneous state in North America in which the past is broken and young people therefore find it an enormous jump to come to that past.

MALIK: Well, it may be that three hundred years, or two hundred years, are about as long a time as is necessary for that experiment to go on. It may be, in fact I think it is, time now for the Western hemisphere to recognize its historical traditional roots. Also it may very well be that the Lockean and Machiavellian criticisms of the great tradition, which occurred outside the unity of Western civilization were [resented] at the time by the church. I go back to the church (I am Greek Orthodox myself), and therefore, I am not much impressed by any reference to Locke, or Machiavelli, or Rousseau. It is these very people who set themselves outside the unity and continuity of the tradition who have brought about the present chaos in which you in the Western world, and all of us (because we all depend on you these days), are living. So what is needed is something of heroic, gigantic magnitude so far as the reformation and reconstruction – I think you used the word reconstitution somewhere – of life and thought and history is concerned. And this task should be done precisely by the new world. So I believe that the real cure is a return. You are quite right in saying there is no return in the identical sense of return. But there is certainly a reconstitution of the unity of the spirit of the tradition. Certainly there is that and that ought to be done. This seems to me to be the most important task facing Western thinkers today.

GPG: Dr Malik, you're a man who came out of the very centre where the original western tradition came from. What was the meaning for you in the church? How did you find the movement of that into the world of politics? You went for your country to the United Nations, you served your country, you have been very much at the centre of the public world, the Western world since 1945. What was the relation of the depth of your philosophic and religious life to that life in the public world?

MALIK: Well, I am very grateful to you for that question. I've found absolutely no discontinuity, no contradiction, between being a religious person, which I always was, and serving as best I could under the general world diplomatic conditions under which I worked. If we are thrown in this life we struggle in it to the best of our ability. I don't believe at any time I subordinated the ultimate truths of the spirit or used them for any political purpose whatsoever. They stood uppermost in my mind and I could apply them here and there as occasion offered to the best of my ability.

GPG: Can I ask you about this, Dr Malik? You did this as a citizen of a civilized country, a non-aggressive country, a fairly small country. Do you think you could have done it in the service of one of the powerful, aggressive, violent empires? On the one hand, obviously you couldn't have done it as a Christian for the Soviet Union because its empire is ruled by a very hostile view of the spirit. If I may talk about my own life and a lot of the young people's lives, the Vietnam War was, for us, an enormous break in the sense that one felt that one could no longer do it for North America, that North America was proving itself a more violent empire [and] was entering the lists of competition. Would it have been possible for you to do this if you had been a citizen of a great and powerful empire in the modern world?

MALIK: Well, it's obvious that it is impossible to answer that question because I don't know whether I would have been able to do it, nor do I know whether were I a citizen for such an empire, as you put it, that that empire would have asked me to do for it what I was asked to do for that little country to which you referred. But I don't share this sense of guilt on your part and on the part of many of the young these days about Vietnam and about many other things in the Western world to the extent to which some of you seem to have it. I respect your feeling, but I think there is a great deal of unnaturalness and sentimentality about it. There is a great deal of going over to the other side. There are two ways of reacting, my friend. There are always two ways of doing anything – the right way and the wrong way. And to react in the manner in which your youth now and many of your older folks are reacting by doubting your deepest values is the wrong way. Regardless of the rights and wrongs of the war, as I said, if young people or thinkers in the Western world react against the thing, there are two ways of reacting against it: one way would be to go all the way over to the position of your opponents, and that is what is happening in the minds of many soft-headed people. They're all Ho Chi-Minhists; they're all marxists now just to spite their own people, their own government, their own tradition. That seems to me to be the wrong reaction to a situation even if the reaction were justified in the first place. The best way to react to a situation is to go back to your deepest values, [values] that are different from what your youthful rebels are stating these days. I find them becoming denatured reacting against the war in Vietnam and going all the way over to the values of the people whom you are fighting in Vietnam and that

I don't think is healthy at all. I think it's superficial, sentimental, childish, and you'll get over it.

GPG: I think it's not only wrong, but extremely foolish to think that you can ever have, or should want, or it would do any good to have, a left-wing revolution on this continent. But on the other hand, to a lot of the young people, it would be the established powers of North America who have denied the tradition. Compared to what General Motors, General Electric, and people like that are doing in denaturing people, the reaction of the left is very minor on this continent.

MALIK: Now let me make one point clear. I do not intend to make any statement about the Vietnam War. There are two ways of reacting against anything. One way is to say that that thing is bad because it is founded on bad principles. But then whoever says that must tell us what his principles are and the principles of your youthful reactors today are not better *at all* than the principles against which they are reacting. That is what I am saying.

GPG: But is it not true that the principles against which they are reacting are not [those of] the great Western tradition? They are [reacting against] slick modern twentieth-century liberalism. Surely these protestors at their best may be reacting against an extraordinary emptiness of tradition in North American society. I mean, after all, one of the men being tried in Chicago, Mr Hoffman, defined American liberalism as, 'God is dead and we did it for the kids.' It's against this emptiness of tradition that a lot of the youngsters, I think, are reacting.

MALIK: I wish they were reacting in the name of Jesus Christ of Nazareth, which is the last thing they would think of. They would much rather think of Uncle Ho. They have not gone deep into their own tradition. If they reacted in the name of the tradition I would not only respect them, I would go along with them. But if they react in terms of an imported, improvised, synthetic view of life that is so vague, and so unreal, and so alien, I don't respect them.

GPG: What do you think will happen to the church when it ceases to hold the established powers of the Western world?

MALIK: Well, it will be tried: it will be persecuted; it will go back to the catacombs; it will suffer; it will be crucified, but it will rise on the third day as it always did in the past. The church will never disappear; all else will disappear. How many cultures and civilizations have disappeared? I see no reason why Canadian civilization is not going to disappear. It could disappear – it is not much greater than all those cultures that disappeared, but I see every reason why the church is going to survive Canadian civilization. And Canadian civilization can survive only to the extent that it can hitch its wagon to the star of the church. This I see very clearly, so clearly that it is more true to me than any mathematical proposition.

GPG: But out of that Western tradition, centred on Western Christianity, there has come forth this dynamic civilization that has at least at a public level or an official level dug the grave of that from which it came forth.

MALIK: Yes, well, it will never dig the grave of the church, of course; it digs its own grave, and, well, all right. Part of the freedom of man is that he can commit suicide. If Western civilization wants to commit suicide, well that's part of its freedom. God will never take that away from it. God is incapable of taking our freedom away from us. *Incapable.* We are responsible. I am responsible, you are responsible, Western civilization is responsible, responsible before God and I hope there will come out of the present deep questioning that you represent and that many others represent and that I deeply feel as I travel about in North America and in Europe, I hope there will come out a tremendous new revival of the spirit in the Western world. We shall always have dying, stupid civilizations. We shall always have kingdoms of men that will disintegrate. And we shall always have the church of Christ that will never disappear until He comes again.